London

Select

contents

London overview

Ever since the Romans came, saw and expanded a small Saxon town on the banks of the Thames naming it Londinium, Britain's capital has excelled at changing and growing, two things it has not stopped doing for two millennia.

The English historian and scholar Edward Gibbon said of London in the 18th century: 'it is an astonishing and perpetual spectacle'. And, although it's no longer the biggest city in the world nor the centre of a huge British empire, London is still a vast and vibrant 24-hour show. A place where you can: watch buskers on the South Bank and groundbreaking theatre at the Donmar; see soldiers in bearskin hats performing ancient rituals in front of Buckingham Palace and inline skaters doing their exuberant thing to a hip hop beat in Hyde Park; view Victorian bustles in the V&A costume hall and a parade of the latest fashion tribes at Brick Lane market.

It is also no exaggeration to say it's a world in one city. London has always thrived on a continuous flow of immigrants who contribute in untold ways to its cultural life without changing its quintessentially British nature. Many of the Michelin stars now awarded to London chefs are not just for imaginative British cuisine, but also for massala dosas and dim sum. London may no longer be the world's most important port, but it has found other ways to be world-leading. The once run-down part of east London, Hoxton, has become Europe's premier modern art market.

Where many cities are pickled in aspic, London keeps adding spectacular new buildings to its canon. The upstart London Eye has been standing just over a decade, but it has already made a huge impact on how visitors view the city, both literally and figuratively. Along with other relative newcomers to the horizon – the 'Gherkin', City Hall, Tate Modern and the Millennium Bridge – it's made London a fun place again. And the arrival of all the exciting new stadia in the Olympic city can only further build on this new-found confidence and vibrancy. Enjoy!

in the mood for...

... street life

Britons are widely regarded as being rather reserved, but British street life has always been very lively. And so it is that a city where everybody obediently stands to the right on the escalator is also the birthplace of punk and the cradle of wildly inventive designers like Vivienne Westwood, John Galliano and the late Alexander McQueen. If you want to observe the next flowering of British street style hang around the **Seven Dials** *(p.62)* where Central St Martins fashion students are to be seen rocking their latest creations, or **Brick Lane** *(p.108)* where many fledgling designers are setting up new stalls and shops. Markets are also excellent for people/style-watching – try **Camden** *(p.161)* for rocker types; **Portobello** *(p.160)* for boho beauties, and **Broadway Market** *(p.165)* for the art tribe. London also has great street art and performance. The tube has licensed buskers in 22 central stations, and during any walk on the **South Bank** *(p.128)*, you will be serenaded by musicians of every genre. Perhaps the best spot to watch London street life is outside **Bar Italia** *(p.48)*.

... fine dining

Britain is still behind France and Italy for Michelin stars, but London's constellation, which increases most years, has helped to establish and strengthen the country's reputation as a gastro *tour de force* – and Mayfair has the highest concentration of Michelin-starred restaurants in London. Take your pick *(p.34)*.

If you want to understand how traditional British cooking became great again, **St John** *(p.106)* is the go-to place. There are few parts of the animal, from intestines to bone marrow, that haven't found their way onto a plate in this renowned restaurant. And at **Hix** *(p.50)* you can see another chef (the eponymous Mark) in his prime reinventing classic British dishes such as meat pies or sand dabs and making them lighter, and more inventive and delicious, than they sound. At **Wild Honey** *(p.34)* you can find the best the UK and mainland Europe have to offer – Cornish gurnard, Limousin lamb, Spanish chorizo – in many fabulous plates. Innovative spicing and exquisite curries from across India reward the British love of Indian food with a very classy curry house at **Benares** *(p.34)*.

... retail therapy

You cannot discuss shopping in London without mentioning the holy trinity of **Harrods** *(p.142)*, **Harvey Nichols** *(p.142)* and **Selfridges** *(pictured, p.40)*. But there is so much more to London's shopping scene than department stores. It has several high streets – in **Marylebone** *(p.38)*, **Richmond** *(p.166)* and **Islington** *(p.162)* – that showcase the best of the British chains along with funkier little independent stores. Then there are the speciality areas such as **Borough** *(p.127)* for food, **Charing Cross Road** *(p.57)* for books, **Mount Street** *(p.35)* for couture, **Denmark Street** for musical instruments, **Brick Lane** *(p.108)* and **Portobello** *(p.160)* for vintage, **Newburgh Street** *(p.51)* for cutting-edge fashion, **Bermondsey** *(p.133)* and **Islington** *(p.162)* for antiques. Plus a handsome smattering of

one-of-a-kind, only-in-London shops such as **Fortnum & Mason** *(p.33)*, **Liberty** *(p.51)*, **Geo F. Trumper** *(p.36)*, **Savile Row** *(p.37)* and **James Smith & Sons** *(p.99)*. Markets, both open-air and covered, are also very important – thousands flock to **Spitalfields** *(p.116)*, **Camden** *(p.161)* and **Broadway** *(p.165)* every week in search of fresh foods and smart fashions. And museum shops have come a long way from the dusty postcard and mug days – the retail spaces of the **British Museum** *(p.92)*, the **British Library** *(p.89)* and **Tate Modern** *(p.130)* are particularly noteworthy for their range of books, jewellery and objets that you would not encounter anywhere else. The **Science Museum** *(p.144)* has a range of toys that knocks Hamleys into a cocked hat.

... a night on the town

Whether you want to put a Shakespearean play, an experimental drama, a heavy metal or indie band, a Hollywood blockbuster or an opera as the central entertainment to your big night out, London will have it in abundance. Just for starters for the list above, you could go to: **The Globe** (p.131), **The National** (p.135), **The Barbican** (p.112), **the Donmar** (p.56), **the Almeida** (p.162), **Barfly**, (p.161), **The 100 Club** (p.59), **The Curzon** (p.41) or the **Royal Opera House** (p.53). For a drink beforehand, try the bar in the **St Martin's Lane** (p.175) or the crypt of **St Martin-in-the-Fields** (p.71). For a meal afterwards, walk into

Chinatown (p.55) for something quick, cheap and delicious, or go for the full after-theatre splendour of **The Ivy** (p.60). Or for something somewhere in between try **Wahaca** (p.60), a lively, jumping joint with marvellous Mexican street food and terrific Tequila-based cocktails.

If it's a glamorous, no expenses spared night out you have in mind, why not precede dinner in a gastronomic temple (p.7) with a cocktail at the **Coburg** (p.42) or a plush Kensington bar (p.153)? Or keep it simple and low-key and while away an evening nursing a drink or two in a good old-fashioned boozer – or gastro-pub if you want some food to soak up the alcohol (p. 31, p.50).

... romance

A heartstopping view is a prerequisite for any romantic interludes so start with a stroll by the Serpentine, the stretch of water that runs between Hyde Park and Kensington Gardens, and perhaps a meander through the lovely **Serpentine Gallery** *(p.150)* sculpture garden. There is no place more romantic for lunch than the **Orangery in Holland Park** *(p.160)* or you could go for one with a view at **Galvin at Windows** *(p.34)*. Then a spot of sightseeing at **St Paul's** *(p.110)*, the fairy-tale setting of the wedding of Prince Charles and Lady Diana. Cross the **Millennium Bridge** and take a river walk *(p.128)* to the London Eye, where the seriously romantic can get a capsule to themselves for around £450. **Hakkasan** *(p.55)* where dim sum is given the full glamour treatment is a very romantic setting for dinner. A glass of champagne with a hint of Parisian adventures at **St Pancras** *(p.90)* would round things off nicely, and if you and your beloved are still awake in the wee small hours, watch the sun come up over the big city from **Parliament Hill** *(p.167)*.

... family fun

Britons are relatively reserved in their relations to children and don't make such a big fuss of them as continental Europeans, but while formal restaurants might ask them to shush, children can have a fantastic time in the big smoke. Classy chain restaurants like **Giraffe** on the South Bank (*p.134*), **fish!** at Borough (*p.127*), or **Carluccios** and **Pizza Express** all over town provide paper, puzzles and pencils to small diners. The **Museum of Childhood** (*p.163*) is an obvious choice, but most of London's museums have activities for kids – the art trolley at **Tate Britain** (*p.72*), hands-on tables at the **British Museum** (*p.92*) and magic carpet stories at the **National Gallery** (*p.68*) are huge fun. The **Science Museum** (*p.144*) with all its interactive exhibits is always a hit. London's parks are a godsend when they need a run around. Most have playgrounds, but the best outdoor play space by a mile is the **Diana Princess of Wales memorial playground** (*p.150*). And if they've behaved themselves, treat them to ice cream from **Oddono's** (*p.143*).

in the mood for...

... a quintessential London experience

Ask what the quintessential London experience is, and you'll get as many answers as people you ask. It could be: a hearty breakfast 'fry-up' at **Smith's of Smithfield** *(p.106)*; a dainty lunch in stately surrounds at **The Wallace Collection** *(p.28)*, **Tate Britain** *(p.72)* or the **National Dining Rooms** *(p.68)*; fish and chips among taxi drivers at the **Fryer's Delight** *(p.98)*, a walk in the rain, or a cheese and pickle sandwich on a park bench gazing at the rose garden in **Regent's Park** *(p.86)*, or a ride to the West End in a black cab or on a red **Routemaster bus** *(p.118)*. Then again it is probably tea at the **Orangery** *(p.151)* or hearing that announcement on the tube 'Mind the gap' for the first time. No, hang on, it's dinner at **Rules** *(p.60)*. No, no, no, it's a warm pint at **The Coach and Horses** *(p.50)* ...

... history

The river Thames is both the reason London was settled and an explanation of how it went on to become one of the world's largest and most influential cities. So, walking along its banks is a great way of tapping into the city's past (*p.128*). The **Museum of London** (*p.115*) enables you to absorb more of this history in its galleries, and the best slices of living history are to be found at the **Imperial War Museum** (*p.137*), the **Cabinet War Rooms** (*p.77*) and the evocative **Dennis Severs House** (*pictured; p.117*).

... a lazy day

The deckchairs in London's parks are like mini hammocks in which to slouch, chill and watch the world go by. The **Electric Cinema** (*p.41*) has sofas for two in the auditorium and a bar with sofas on which snacks can be brought to you. Or catch a movie at the **BFI** (*p.135*) and recline in one of the leather sofas at Benugo afterwards. Sunday lunch is a fine British tradition, as is the habit of taking root in an armchair with a paper and a drink – great locations for this include **Great Queen Street** (*p.61*), **Only Running Footman** (*p.31*) and **The Garrison** (*p.133*).

... being pampered

Most of London's swisher hotels such as **Claridges** *(p.172)* or the **Soho Hotel** *(p.178)* have in-room massage, and a lot of them such as **The Sanderson** *(p.177)*, the **Berkeley** *(p.154)*, **Browns** *(p.173)* and the **Mandarin Oriental** *(p.172)* have spas where you can get lost on a cloud of fragrance and steam. Or just give your feet a treat and walk them to the pedicure room at **Fortnum & Mason** *(p.33)* to be soothed and beautified. For organic beauty products, soothing therapies and remedies in a relaxed, hippyish atmosphere, go to **Neal's Yard** *(p.62)*.

... being sporty in the great outdoors

The fact that London is full of parks and green spaces probably has not escaped your attention, but when you are looking for routes to run, jog or power-walk, you should also consider the river and **canal tow paths** (Camden to Little Venice is a lovely stretch). For a more 'wilderness' run, head for **Richmond Park** *(p.166)* or **Hampstead Heath** *(p.167)* which also has pools for open-air swimming in summer. Those with wheels can join inline skaters near the boathouse at the Serpentine in **Hyde Park** *(p.150)*.

... royalty

There are palaces with royal pomp and splendour aplenty in London, not just Buckingham Palace, but the **Tower of London** *(p.114)*, **Kensington Palace** *(p.151)* and **Banqueting House** *(p.76)* have all housed and feted crowned heads. And almost all of the big parks – Hyde, Regent's and St James's – were royal hunting grounds, but the most beautiful of these is the one with deer still in it at **Richmond** *(p.166)*. However, house and garden aren't the only ways of channelling royalty – you could shop like them too and become a patron of one of the many shops with royal warrants *(see box on p.33)*; you can even shop at the Queen's bra shop, Rigby & Peller, just around the corner from **Harrods** *(p.142)*. Or bop like a royal in **Mahiki** *(p.42)* where the young Princes sometimes spend an evening.

... something free

If you took two well-known sayings: 'the best things in life are free', and 'If you are tired of London you are tired of life', and put them together, you could have a pretty good time. Here's how: all the national art galleries and museums are free although they encourage donations; if you wander the galleries of **Hoxton** and **Shoreditch** (p.164) on a Thursday evening you could be invited in to a private view and given a glass of wine. There are free lunchtime concerts in London churches such as those at **St James's Piccadilly** (p.43) and free foyer events almost every day in the **Southbank Centre** (p.134). And if you wander **Borough Market** (pictured; p.127) you will be amazed at how much free food you are invited to try.

... literary inspirations

The obvious place to seek literary associations is the **British Library** *(p.89)* where modern authors can be seen researching, along with the work of thousands of others stretching back to William Blake's notebooks or beyond to the medieval Luttrell Psalter. In **Bloomsbury** and the **South Bank**, you can barely move without touching something once touched by Shakespeare *(p.131)* or Dickens *(p.96)*. Or head for **Hampstead** *(p.167)* once a magnet for writers and intellectuals, to pay tribute to Keats and Freud. Bibliophiles should not miss a visit to **Charing Cross Road** *(p.57)* or the giant **Waterstone's** on Piccadilly *(p.43)*.

... modern architecture

The metropolis is best known as a repository of ancient buildings and grand old palaces, but it also has many marvels of modern architecture. These include: the **Olympic Village** *(p.163)*, and its centrepiece the Aquatic Centre by Zaha Hadid, Sir Norman Foster's 30 St Mary Axe, better known as the '**Gherkin**' *(p.111)* and his **City Hall** on the opposite bank, by Tower Bridge, Sir Richard Rogers' **Lloyd's Building** *(p.111)*, the **Millennium Bridge** *(p.128)* and the much-loved **London Eye** *(p.129)*.

neighbourhoods

The Thames wiggles through the centre of greater London, but it is at the bottom of central London. The only bit of London south of the Thames visited by millions of visitors is the South Bank. North of the river, London is divided into the two cities of Westminster and The City, representing the cultural and financial centres respectively.

Mayfair and Marylebone Marylebone, defined by Oxford Street to the south and Marylebone Road to the north, is a discreet residential area of Edwardian apartment blocks with a delightful high street. Mayfair is bounded by Park Lane and Regent Street and bisected by Bond Street. It is London's most blue-blooded area peopled by the gentility and peppered with Michelin-starred restaurants, grand hotels, couture stores and classic shops.

Soho and Covent Garden Soho and Covent Garden, with their abundance of shops, restaurants and theatres, are the twin hubs of tourist London, but if you step back from their overcrowded centres – Piccadilly Circus, Leicester Square, Oxford Street and Covent Garden Piazza – you are in the chic and lively heart of the West End.

Westminster and St James's To many, Westminster and St James's are central London. Between them they have the highest concentration of iconic buildings – the Houses of Parliament, Big Ben, Westminster Abbey, 10 Downing Street, Buckingham Palace, Trafalgar Square – not to mention the National Galleries and St James's Park.

Bloomsbury and Holborn Bloomsbury is best known for its literary connections. Once the home of Virginia Woolf, E.M. Forster and Britain's publishing houses, it is still a thriving cultural area thanks to the presence of University College London and the British Museum. Made up of Georgian terraces with beautiful green squares, Bloomsbury and Holborn are pleasingly quiet areas to wander around.

City, Clerkenwell and Spitalfields The City, or the Square Mile as it is also known, stands on the original settled area of London, and is now the financial district. Thus thrusting glass and steel bank headquarters nestle against centuries-old churches and pubs. The warehouses and print shops of old Clerkenwell are now the loft spaces, bars and clubs of its stylish new inhabitants. Dedicated fashion followers and bargain hunters flock east to the markets and boutiques of Spitalfields and Brick Lane.

The South Bank The South Bank is the south side of the river between Tower and Westminster bridges. If you only had time for one slice of London sightseeing, make it this. Here in microcosm you have the best of London: fantastic food (Borough), art (Tate Modern), theatre (Shakespeare's Globe and the National), music (Royal Festival Hall) and architecture (Tower Bridge and the London Eye).

Kensington and Chelsea Kensington, Chelsea and Knightsbridge are the most traditional, least changing parts of the city. Largely residential, the quiet squares and immaculate terraced housing are civilised, genteel pockets broken up by the posh shopping streets of Knightsbridge and the Kings Road, and the museum mile of Brompton and Exhibition Roads.

Village London London is not a homogeneous city. It is rather a chaotic patchwork of overlapping villages all of which have distinctly different characters – boho Notting Hill, edgy Camden, easy Islington, gritty East End, arty Hoxton, intellectual Hampstead, scientific Greenwich and green Richmond – all merit a visit.

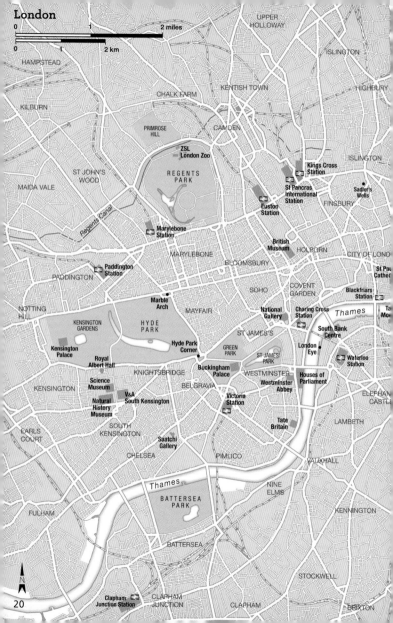

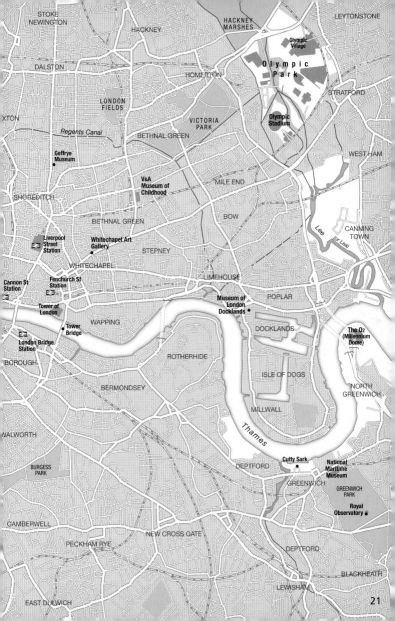

Mayfair and Marylebone

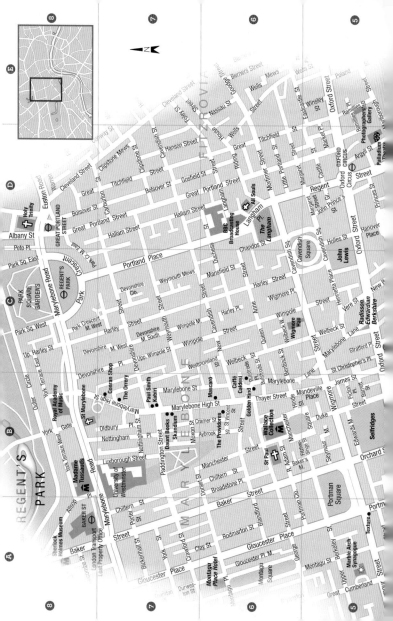

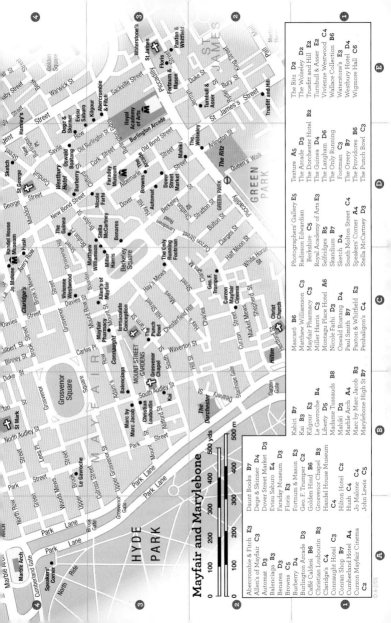

Mayfair and Marylebone

Abercrombie & Fitch **E3**	
Allen's of Mayfair **C3**	
Automat **D3**	
Balenciaga **B3**	
Benares **D3**	
Browns **C5**	
Burberry **D4**	
Burlington Arcade **D4**	
Caffè Caldesi **B6**	
Christian Louboutin **B3**	
Claridge's **C4**	
Connaught Hotel **C3**	
Conran Shop **B7**	
Cumberland Hotel **A4**	
Curzon Mayfair Cinema **C2**	

Daunt Books **B7**	
Dege & Skinner **D4**	
Dover Street Market **D3**	
Evisu Saburo **E4**	
Faraday Museum **D3**	
Floris **E3**	
Fortnum & Mason **E3**	
Geo. F. Trumper **C2**	
Golden Hind **B6**	
Grosvenor Chapel **B3**	
Handel House Museum **C4**	
Hilton Hotel **C2**	
Hush **C4**	
Jo Malone **C4**	
John Lewis **C5**	

Kabiri **B7**	
Kai **B3**	
Kilgour **E3**	
Le Gavroche **B4**	
Liberty **D5**	
Madame Tussauds **B8**	
Mahiki **D3**	
Marble Arch **A4**	
Marc by Marc Jacob **B3**	
Marylebone High St **B7**	

Mascaró **B6**	
Matthew Williamson **C3**	
Mayfair Pharmacy **C3**	
Miller Harris **C3**	
Montagu Place Hotel **A6**	
Nicole Farhi **D3**	
Oswald Boatang **D4**	
Paul Smith **B7**	
Paxton & Whitfield **E3**	
Penhaligon's **C4**	

Photographers' Gallery **E5**	
Radisson Edwardian	
Berkshire **C5**	
Royal Academy of Arts **E3**	
Selfridges **B5**	
Skandium **B7**	
Sketch **D4**	
South Molton Street **C4**	
Speakers' Corner **A4**	
Stella McCartney **C4**	

Texture **A5**	
The Arcade **D3**	
The Dorchester Hotel	
The Guinea **D4**	
The Langham **D6**	
The Only Running	
Footman **E3**	
The Orrery **C7**	
The Providores **B6**	
The Punch Bowl **C3**	

The Ritz **D2**	
The Wolseley **D2**	
Truefitt and Hill **E2**	
Turnbull & Asser **E2**	
Vivienne Westwood **C4**	
Wallace Collection **B6**	
Waterstone's **E3**	
Westbury Hotel **D4**	
Wigmore Hall **C6**	

Breakfast in style at The Wolseley, a palatial café in the grand European tradition

Previously breakfast choices in Britain's capital were more or less limited to the greasy fry-up of the working man's café or the bland buffet of the big hotel. That has all changed and there's now a wide range of places providing seriously good options (*see box*). And there's nowhere better to breakfast in style than the Wolseley: a glimmering, shimmering place full of marble, chandeliers, chinoiserie and old-world elegance that make it feel more like a palace than a former car showroom (it was built in the 1920s by Wolseley Motor Company). But the thing that really makes the Wolseley such an attractive place to have any meal is its lively social energy – it's a magnet to the fashion, media, art and business crowds. Restaurant critics have devoted acres of print to the perfection of the porridge here. Those less enamoured of oatmeal can opt for prunes with orange and ginger, kippers, Greek yoghurt and fruit salad, French toast, a full English, or, for the more brave, Haggis and duck egg.

The Wolseley, 160 Piccadilly; tel: 020 7499 6996; Mon–Fri 7am–midnight, Sat 9am–midnight, Sun 9am–11pm; www.thewolseley.com; map D2

GREAT PLACES FOR BREAKFAST
The Albion Café at the **Boundary** hotel (*p.177*) has traditional British in trendy, arty surroundings; **Automat** (33 Dover St; tel: 020 7499 3033; map D3) for American morning delights; **Canteen** at Baker Street, Spitalfields or South Bank (*p.135*) for all-day breakfast; The **Cinnamon Club** (*p.74*) for something delicately spiced; **The Fox & Anchor** (*p.107*) in Smithfield for a meaty breakfast with a Guinness; **The National** (*p.68*) to combine it with sightseeing; **York & Albany** (127–129 Parkway; tel: 020 7388 3344) by Regent's Park for a hearty one to prepare you for a good walk; and if money's no object, **Simpson's-in-the-Strand** (*p.60*).

Go to a **Sunday morning concert** in the Art Deco splendour of the **Wigmore Hall**

Sunday mornings when you are on a short break can be problematic – on the one hand it's Sunday so you want to take it easy. On the other, you are in an exciting big city and it's a shame to do nothing. If you are on the horns of this dilemma or need something to fill in a few precious pre-lunch hours, you could do a lot worse than attend a morning concert at the Wigmore Hall. They are held at 11am every Sunday. The concerts and recitals by a range of celebrated chamber music groups last an hour and there is a free glass of sherry or cup of coffee for all afterwards.

Originally called the Bechstein Hall, this concert hall is both impressive and intimate. It was built in 1910 by the German piano firm which had showrooms next door, but with the outbreak of war in 1914 came hostility to anything German-sounding and it was seized as enemy property. It was sold off for a song (to the nearby Debenhams Department Store) and reopened in 1917 as the Wigmore Hall. Thanks to its near-perfect acoustics, it has gone on to become one of the world's leading recital venues. Over the years many famous composers and musicians have performed here, from Arthur Rubinstein, Benjamin Britten and Jacqueline du Pré to András Schiff and Joshua Bell. There are events for children on Saturday called Chamber Tots, and the restaurant in the basement does a reasonable Sunday lunch.

The Wigmore Hall, 36 Wigmore St; tel: 020 7935 2141; www.wigmore-hall.org. uk; map C6

Take in superb works of **18th-century art** set in an exquisite town house at the **Wallace Collection**

If you fear you are getting art and/or museum burnout, it might be time for a small gem of a museum like the Wallace Collection to revive your interests. Failing that, just go straight to the beautiful tranquil café in the atrium where you can have breakfast, lunch or afternoon tea, and that should do the trick of restoring you to good spirits. The Wallace Collection is set in a stunning town house in Manchester Square tucked away just yards from the teeming crowds of Oxford Street. It houses the personal collection of 17th- and 18th-century art, made by the Marquesses of Hertford and Sir Richard Wallace, and bequeathed to the nation by his widow in the 19th century. It has been open free to the public ever since.

Even if you think you have no interest in 17th- and 18th-century art, you will find many works to savour, not a few of which you may already know such as Rembrandt's *Self Portrait in a Black Cap*, Hals's *The Laughing Cavalier (pictured)*, Fragonard's *The Swing*, and the poignant *Edward V and the Duke of York in the Tower* by Delaroche.

The Wallace is a beautiful formal space, but not at all stuffy,

and kids love it especially when they find the small room at the back of the ground floor in which they are allowed to touch replicas from the collection and try on one of the suits of armour.

The Wallace Collection, Hertford House, Manchester Square; tel: 020 7563 9500; daily 10am–5pm; free; www.wallacecollection.org; map B6

Forage for **great fashion finds** in and around **South Molton Street**

If you quizzed people at random as to who the most influential woman in British fashion is, they would come up with many names – Anna Wintour? Suzy Menkes? Vivienne Westwood? – before they came up with 'Joan Burstein'. Yet Mrs B, as she is affectionately known, is responsible for introducing the British fashion-buying public to Giorgio Armani, Donna Karan, Comme des Garcons, Sonia Rykiel, Azzedine Alaia, John Galliano, Alexander McQueen, Hussein Chalayan, Jil Sander – everybody really. And she has done it all with a brilliant eye for talent spotting and inspired, eclectic buying for her boutique, **Browns** (23–27 and 38–39 South Molton St; map C5). Over the 40 years they've been here, Mrs B and Browns have revolutionised South Molton Street, a lovely Georgian street, turning it into a pedestrian haven full of great fashion finds (*pictured here at Christmas time*).

A short walk away is the flagship store of French-born designer **Nicole Farhi** (158 New Bond St; map D3), who made her name in the UK. It has womenswear, menswear and home furnishings, all of which are good, but best of all in this area short of good, casual places to eat, it has a very relaxed

and stylish café, **Nicole's**. It's a great place to park your carrier bags and break from shopping for lunch. Emerge re-energised and hit the six exciting floors of stripped-down industrial space turned trendy fashion department store at **Dover St Market** (17–18 Dover St; tel: 020 7518 0680; map D3). The brainchild of Rei Kawakubo, designer at Comme des Garcons, it showcases the brightest talents, emerging and established, from around the world. The design-forward outlets include Givenchy, Celine, Norse Project, Christopher Kane and Proenza Schouler.

South Molton Street; map C5–6

Journey through Handel's life in the powerfully evocative **Handel House Museum**

You arrive in the Handel House Museum through a bright, ultra-modern courtyard, take a lift to the top of the house, open a door marked 'museum', and then are hurtled, Alice-like, into another world. Suddenly you have stepped back into Georgian London. Well, we are saying that, but there is actually an audiovisual presentation about the remarkably thorough renovation of this house where George Frideric Handel lived and worked for 36 years, but it takes a while to spot the screen in the midday gloom (the house is lit to simulate the pre-electric age) and you don't have to watch the newfangled thing if you want to stay in the mood. The walls are painted in the dark, dirt-concealing colours popular in his day; the restorers peeled back the layers of paint until they got to the original dark grey and then made an exact match. They have done the same trick with the furnishings, working from the inventory made when he died here in his bed in 1759. And then they have adorned the walls with paintings of Handel, his friends and London in his day, and placed his instruments and manuscripts artfully about the place. For added atmosphere, the house is often alive with music (see website for details of recitals and harpsichord workshops). It all adds up to a fascinating and evocative portrait of a genius at work, and a man in his time. Visitors, especially the younger ones, are encouraged to try on Georgian costumes and compose their own masterpieces.

The museum also owns 23 Brook Street, where, centuries later, Jimi Hendrix lived, and they have dedicated a room to him and his distinctly different lifestyle.

Handel House Museum, 25 Brook St; tel: 020 7495 1685; www.handelhouse.org; map C4

Prop up the bar decorously and enjoy a pint in the lovely old-world boozers of Mayfair

Tucked away down a quaint little mews off Berkeley Square, **The Guinea** (30 Bruton Place; tel: 020 7409 1728; map D4) is a reminder of days gone by in a part of Mayfair that gleams with glass and steel modernity. Dating back to the 15th century, The Guinea is small, dark and atmospheric. It has Young's beer and steak and kidney pies; certainly not the gourmet fare more common in these parts, but definitely of a high standard.

The Only Running Footman (5 Charles St; tel: 020 7499 2988; map C3) is a pretty pub that looks more

like it should be on the edge of a village green than slap-bang in the middle of a city. Downstairs the bar is mostly filled with a lively, boisterous crowd, especially on weekend lunch times. Upstairs the dining room is more subdued and elegant. The food is traditional pub food – such as a choice of three roasts, Morecambe Bay potted shrimp, burgers, fish cakes with poached eggs, and some handsome puddings and pies – but done well and with a lighter than usual touch.

Built in the 1730s, **The Punch Bowl** (41 Farm St; tel: 020 7493 6841; map C3) is the second-oldest pub in Mayfair, but as it is now part-owned by film director Guy Ritchie, people are much more interested in its celebrity-spotting potential than its history. Which is a shame because whatever its patronage it is still just a lovely old pub with bare floorboards, panelled walls and, oh okay, Guy Ritchie has been seen in here with his friends Jude Law, Leonardo Di Caprio, Beyonce, Jay-Z and Justin Timberlake. He also occasionally appears in the pub's house band. But, honestly, the main attraction really is the good range of ales and decent (if slightly higher priced than usual) pub food.

Take in a **major exhibition** then digest it in the airy modern café at the **Royal Academy of Arts**

An abiding tradition of the Royal Academy is that whenever an artist is elected as a member, they are required to donate a work typical of their style. This amazing yet little-known collection includes bequests from Joshua Reynolds, Turner, Constable, Hockney and Tracey Emin. Highlights from the collection can be seen on free 1-hour tours (1pm Tue–Fri, 3pm Wed–Fri, and 11.30am Sat) of the John Madejski Fine Rooms.

But the Academy is best known for another of its founding principles, 'to mount an annual exhibition open to all artists of distinguished merit', which it has done every year since 1769. Now known as the Summer Exhibition (it runs from June to mid-August) it gets around 10,000 submissions a year from which the Academicians make their final pick of 1,200 works. And then there are the headline-grabbing showcase exhibitions such as 1997's Sensation featuring the YBAs (Young British Artists) that brought protestors and picketers along with throngs curious to see what all the fuss was about. Or the Anish Kapoor exhibition in 2009 in which a cannon shot red wax into a room of this beautiful old gallery at regular intervals.

More recently, the Academy has applied the idea of the temporary installation to its restaurant as well as its galleries, hosting a series of pop-up restaurants. Flash, the first, was a cool and buzzy room made of art packing cases. Then quirky Mayfair restaurant **Sketch** *(p.34)* took up residence for a while. Who knows who'll be there at the time of your visit, but it is worth checking out. As is the Norman Foster-designed café for light snacks.

Royal Academy of Arts, Burlington House, Piccadilly; tel: 020 7300 8000; www.royalacademy.org.uk; map E3

Be treated royally at **Fortnum and Mason**, the **Queen's grocer**

As you might imagine in a store where impeccably polite staff still wear tailcoats, its credentials are very impressive. In 1761 Charles Fortnum, grandson of the co-founder, went into the service of Queen Charlotte, winning it a Royal Warrant *(see box below)* that is proudly displayed above the shop doors to this day. The store went on to become official suppliers of preserved foods to British Officers during the Napoleonic Wars, catered for state functions at the Court of Queen Victoria, and shipped beef tea to Florence Nightingale's hospitals during the Crimean War. At around this time, Fortnum's (as it is commonly known) also began to supply luxury picnics to high society. These hampers became so popular that Charles Dickens wrote of a day at the races: 'Look where I will.... I see Fortnum & Mason. All the hampers fly wide open and the green downs burst into a blossom of lobster salad!' And it is still a very grand establishment, selling all kinds of delicate items from gentlemen's silk socks to slivers of smoked salmon. But despite this posh pedigree you can still find a jar of Marmite or mustard or tins of tea or toffees, and relatively cheap and quintessentially English items in this gleaming food hall.

Fortnum & Mason, 181 Piccadilly; tel: 020 7734 8040; map E3

THE ROYAL WARRANTS
Royal Warrants are a mark of recognition to companies that have supplied goods or services for at least five years to HM The Queen (or King). Mayfair and St James's have many shops with the royal warrant, including: raincoat manufacturer, **Burberry** (21–23 New Bond St; map D4); bespoke tailors **Gieves & Hawkes** (Savile Row, map E3); cheesemongers **Paxton & Whitfield Ltd** (93 Jermyn St; map E3); shirtmaker **Turnbull & Asser** (71–72 Jermyn St; map E2); hatmakers **James Lock & Co Ltd** (6 St James's St; map E2); and bootmakers **John Lobb Ltd** (9 St James's St; map E2).

Enjoy **fine dining** in the many-starred **restaurants of Mayfair**

Mayfair currently boasts 22 out of the city's total 47 Michelin-starred restaurants. Here is a list of edited highlights for your delectation:

If you want the 'grand French cuisine' experience opt for the three-starred **Alain Ducasse at the Dorchester** (Park Lane, tel: 020 7629 8866; map B2), the two-starred **Le Gavroche** (43 Upper Brook St; tel: 020 7408 0881; map B4), or **Hélène Darroze at the Connaught** (16 Carlos Place, tel: 020 7491 0668; map C3) with one star. One of the newest additions to the galaxy is **Galvin at Windows** (22 Park Lane; tel: 020 7208 4021; map C2) on the 28th floor of the London Hilton, with knockout modern French cuisine and a view to match. There is a slick bar where you can enjoy small plates and the same 180° view. Another place where it works to cheat by sitting at the bar is the modern European restaurant **Texture** (34 Portman St; tel: 020 7224 0028; map A5). Lunches are often a better deal in these highly prized, highly priced places, but at **Sketch** (*pictured*, 9 Conduit St; 020 7659 4500, map D4) you could opt for afternoon tea and get a flavour of its quirky brilliance for around £20. **Wild Honey** (12 St George St; tel: 020 7758 9160; map D4), where old recipes are blended with new technique in flawless, exciting ways, offers lunch and afternoon deals. And proving that London's love of ethnic food can cut across all levels are **Kai** (65 South Audley St; tel: 0872 148 2277; map B3), considered the best Chinese restaurant in London, and **Benares** (12a Berkeley Square House; tel: 020 7629 8866; map D3) for classy contemporary takes on Indian cuisine.

Discover the chicest little **clutch of shops** on **Mount Street**

Commence your fashion walk (head up, hips forward) at the corner of South Audley Street and Mount Street, and you can nip into **Marc by Marc Jacobs** (56 South Audley St) to have a look at the cute lipstick-shaped pens, colourful mesh bags and golden heart-shaped mirrors that they have for £1–3, as it will be the last time you see a price tag like that for a while. Once you turn into Mount Street itself, a beautifully preserved red-brick street in a quiet corner of Mayfair, you will find a cluster of some of fashion's most select names – **Balenciaga** (12), and **Christian Louboutin** (17) who said when he moved here in 2008: 'In this pretty street I want to have my prettiest shoes', and he's not let his shoe-loving fans down on that score. Next comes the **Marc Jacobs** couture store (24–25), opened in 2007. **Vivienne Westwood** (*pictured*) is just around the corner (6 Davies St), as are **Stella McCartney** (30) and **Matthew Williamson** (28) in Bruton Street.

The other end of Mount Street seems to have been preserved in a Victorian bell jar. The **Mayfair Pharmacy** (108), with its enamel and badger-hair shaving brushes lined up in the window, looks exactly as it must have done in the 19th century. And **Allen's of Mayfair** (117) is a 170-year-old butcher's shop, favoured by the many celebrity chefs in the locale.

If you need a secret hideaway after all that commerce, turn into Carlos Place and look for the discreet wrought-iron gated entrance to **Mount Street Gardens**. This is a public park, but it's so tucked away that you can pretty much always have it to yourself. For further respite, there's the **Church of the Immaculate Conception** in the southwest corner of the gardens. Built in 1849 for English Jesuits, it has a particularly lovely high altar by Pugin.

Mount Street; map B3–C3

Get a proper **gentlemanly grooming** at a very **old-world hairdresser** and perfumier

Just walking into this shop is a pleasurable experience redolent of history. The smell of eau de Cologne and bay rum hangs in the air of this Mayfair institution. **Trumper's** was established in 1875 and has been shaving the British elite ever since. And although it has gone on to become a globally recognised brand for the wet-shave enthusiast, the experience is pretty much unchanged. When you walk in you are greeted as Sir or Madam, and if you have a reservation for a cut or shave, the suited receptionist will phone down to the barbers waiting below to tell them to prepare the blades. It is allegedly here that Johnny Depp came to study shaving technique for his role in *Sweeney Todd*. Whether you're after a cut-throat experience – a 20-minute ritual starting with warm towels to open the pores,

and finishing with a discreet touch of moisturiser and a face massage – a quick trim, a pair of moustache trimmers, a badger shaving brush, or just a bottle of shaving lotion or eau de Cologne, Trumper's is the place.

Geo F Trumper, 9 Curzon St; tel: 020 7499 1850; map C2. Or 20 Jermyn St; tel: 020 7724 6553; map E3

THE UNCOMMON SCENTS OF MAYFAIR

Other notable British purveyors of perfume and lotions in the area are: **Ormonde Jayne** (12 The Arcade, 28 Old Bond St; map D3), whose perfumier, Linda Pilkington, specialises in exotic scents; **Miller Harris** (21 Bruton St; map C3), where you can find modern takes on classic fragrances; **Jo Malone** (23 Brook St; map C4), for exotic combinations such as wild fig and cassis, or nutmeg and ginger; and **Penhaligon's** (20A Brook St; map C4), for traditional and classic fragrances. Over in St James's, there is: **Floris** (18 Jermyn St; map E3), for goose-down powder puffs and single-flower fragrances such as Violet and Stephanotis; and **Truefitt & Hill** (71 St James's St; map E2), James Bond's barber, who also has a range of fragrances and products.

Be measured for **exquisite tailoring**, or buy off the peg, in **Savile Row**

The Japanese word for business suit, *sebiro*, is said to be a corruption of Savile Row, and this short street is synonymous worldwide with the artistry and craftsmanship of bespoke tailoring. Even the word 'bespoke' itself was coined here in the 19th century when a particular bolt of cloth was said to 'be spoken for' by a customer for his suit. The tailors here continue to make by hand what are widely considered the best suits in the world, and Savile Row has dressed European aristocracy and royalty, and every icon of male elegance from Nelson to Cary Grant to Jay-Z. A bespoke suit requires four to six fittings, takes five months to complete, and prices start from £3,000 for a two-piece. While the proud tradition of bespoke continues, there is around half the number of bespoke tailors in the Row than there were in the 1980s. The older established firms of the Row – **Henry Poole & Co** (15), **Dege & Skinner** (10), **Kilgour** (5 and 8), **H. Huntsman & Sons** (11) – have had to bow to the pressure of modern times and now also sell made-to-measure and even some off-the-peg ranges. And a newer, sharper modern type of tailor has moved in, as have menswear designers and brands as diverse as **Lanvin** (32) and **Evisu** (9). The new generation on the Row is represented by **Richard James** (29) and **Ozwald Boateng** (30) who, in their separate ways, have managed to infuse traditional tailoring with new colours and fabrics and 'sex up' the image of the Row. In the big building on the corner of Burlington Gardens is **Abercrombie & Fitch**, which, although it sounds like a fitting resident, with its disco ambience and half-naked beefcake bouncers, actually gives the old craftsmen of the Row a fit of the horrors.

Savile Row; map D4

Walk, look, stop, eat, drink and make well-chosen purchases down **Marylebone High Street**

Marylebone High Street has to be one of the world's loveliest shopping streets, a world away from the heaving masses of nearby Oxford Street. It is a near perfect mix of fashion, homeware, food and restaurants with a handful of charity shops where designer bargains can be bagged if you look carefully and time it right.

If your trip includes a Saturday, the best way to experience Marylebone High Street is by starting at **Cabbages and Frocks**, (every Saturday between 11am and 5pm) in the grounds of St Marylebone Parish Church at the Baker Street (northern) end. It is a glorious combination of farmers' market, vintage clothing, cute handmade kids' clothes and homewares. (There is also a food-only Sunday farmers' market.)

The highlights as you walk down Marylebone High Street towards Oxford Street include: **Mascaró** (13) for beautiful Spanish-made shoes and handbags.
Kabiri (37) where the sexy dark walls set off the fun, eclectic one-of-a-kind jewellery ranges perfectly.
Paul Smith (38) which stocks the men's and women's shoe and

accessory collections from the don of British fashion.

The Conran Shop (55), packed full of beautiful objects, and textiles.

The Orrery (55–57; tel: 020 7616 8000) is a great place to meet for a relaxed high-quality lunch. And the rooftop bar is an exceptionally lovely spot to enjoy a Bellini on a warm evening. For flying visits or a snack to go, there is the **Orrery Epicerie** next door.

Apartment C (70) is a lingerie lovers' paradise where they will pour you a drink while you browse the saucy designer and vintage-style underpinnings.

KJ's Laundry (74) has super-stylish womenswear and accessories from designers such as Rebecca Taylor, Ghulam Sakina and Made.

Coco Momo Café Bar (79), a pretty café bar, is a good pre-, post- or during-shopping stop for coffee, lunch, tea and cakes or drinks.

Brora (81) for stylish (ie not your granny's) Scottish cashmere in lovely shades.

Daunt Books (83–84), with its long oak galleries and graceful skylights, is considered by many to be London's most beautiful bookshop.

Skandium (86) for the best of Scandinavian home wares.

Matches (87) stocks exciting youngish brands such as Thakoon, among the more established McQueen, Jacobs and Von Furstenburgs.

Caffe Caldesi (118; tel: 020 7935 1144) has a buzzy, lively caffe downstairs for coffee and cake or beer and snacks, and a more formal restaurant upstairs.

The Providores (109; tel: 020 7935 6175) showcases the prodigious talents of New Zealand-born chef Peter Gordon, while the ground-floor **Tapa Room** is great for breakfast, snacks and drinks.

Marylebone High St; map B6–7

Nurture your love of **vintage wine** in a bar at a **classic London department store**

Selfridges is one of the busiest, and certainly the biggest, of Oxford Street's department stores. So it is a big surprise to find an immaculately understated bar, lining a mezzanine floor overlooking the Wonder Room – the dazzling area dedicated to the most extravagant of luxury goods – making it a marvellous place for people-watching. It is called, of course, the **Wonder Bar**, and in it you can acquaint yourself with some knowledgeable sommeliers and through them some fine vintage wines. There is table service or use the ingenious 'wine juke box' from which you can buy 'sips' – a discreet 25 centilitres – of wine for those wary of forking out for a whole glass. The Wonder Bar has a small menu from the world's artisanal food producers including the *jamons* of Spain, *saucissons* from France and a British cheese plate. And if that gives you an appetite for more, you are well positioned to go and explore Selfridges' wonderful food hall.

Alternatively, if you can still focus, wander off into the well-appointed beauty hall or upstairs to the fashion departments. Selfridges is stocked to the rafters with great clothes. They have a good selection of the mid-price high-street brands such as Jigsaw and Whistles, plus designer-store ranges like Joseph and all the most coveted catwalk designers. And if you are hungry or thirsty (again) there are dozens of in-store mini restaurants and bars to stoke up in.

Selfridges, 400 Oxford Street; tel: 0800 123 400; map B5

Take in an **arthouse film** at London's longest-established independent cinema, **the Curzon**

The Curzon Mayfair is the cinema snob's cinema *par excellence*. It is a million miles from the multiplex experience, and not just because it shows New York Metropolitan Opera Live, is one of the venues for the London Film Festival and has a long pedigree of showing

independent world cinema. No, it also wins prizes for a pleasurable viewing experience with its larger than usual seats, wide auditorium, royal boxes, excellent sound, and a floor pitched 'just so' to ensure you never get anyone's head blocking your view. The crowd is intellectual so you are extremely unlikely to have to suffer people loudly explaining the action or texting their friends or throwing popcorn around.

The Curzon also has stage productions beamed in live from the National Theatre *(p.135)* on Saturday evenings, and themed double bills of old movies on Sundays. The small bar is a lovely place to while away the time before your film starts.

The Curzon Mayfair, 38 Curzon St; tel: 0871 7033 989; map C2

THE BEST CINEMAS IN THE CAPITAL

Launched by Catherine Deneuve in 1998, **Ciné Lumière** (Institut Français, 17 Queensbury Place; tel: 020 7073 1350; map p.140, C5) specialises in French-language films. **The Electric Cinema** (191 Portobello Rd; tel: 020 7908 9696; map p.158, C4) is London's oldest and most elegantly appointed cinema with leather armchairs and two-seat sofas in the auditorium. Luxury hotels **One Aldwych** (map p.47, H4) and **The Charlotte Street Hotel** *(p.174, screening room pictured)* both provide 'dinner and a movie' deals in their plush mini-cinemas. **The Screen on the Green** (83 Upper St, Islington; tel: 0870 0666 4777; map p.159, E4) specialises in Brit cinema. **The Prince Charles** (7 Leicester Square; tel: 0870 811 2559 map p.46, D3) has tickets as low as £1.50 a pop for films no longer on general release.

Enjoy **glamorous cocktails** in some very **elegant bars**

The Coburg Bar at the Connaught (*see p.34*; map C3) has to be one of London's most glamorous drinking places. The palette of jewel colours, the Julian Opie paintings, and the velvet wingbacked chairs make this a truly sumptuous setting to sink into while the bartenders expertly mix you an excellent drink – whisky sours are a speciality. And although cocktails are undeniably expensive, tasty little snacks such as perfect marinated olives and posh hand-cooked crisps arrive unbidden and free of charge to soften the blow.

Meanwhile, **Polo Bar** (The Westbury Hotel, New Bond St; map D4) also manages to avoid all the bland clichés of the hotel bar. It has splendid Art Deco fittings,

a lively post-work crowd, flawless classic cocktails and a generous list of tapas choices for bar food.

Hush (8 Lancashire Court; tel: 020 7659 1500; map C4) is another magical Mayfair location for drinks. The 'boudoir' bar on the first floor is perfect for intimate catch-up chats with your friends over a cool glass of wine.

Mahiki (5–7 Dover St; map D3) is also worth a peek. It is the haunt of younger royals (including Princes William and Harry) so you may be held up a while behind a velvet rope, but once inside this large basement club, you will be rewarded with a surprisingly cool, unbuttoned atmosphere with its faux Hawaiiana, and grass-skirted staff.

Be uplifted by **a beautiful little church** with a big heart

Of the 52 churches that Sir Christopher Wren built in London, **St James's of Piccadilly** was his favourite. It is the only one not to have suffered damage during the Great Fire as it was safely away from the blaze on what were then the outskirts of the city. It wasn't so lucky nearly 300 years later, however, when London was under fire from bombs during the Blitz when it was badly damaged. Fortunately the font and organ case survived intact. They have very fine carvings by Grinling Gibbons, the Dutch-born sculptor who worked with Wren and Inigo Jones.

But this church is better known for its inclusive attitude than its beauty. It has a café at its side which is a tranquil place for a coffee or light lunch, and there are free lunch-time concerts (Mon, Wed and Fri). Out front there is a bustling arts, crafts and antiques market (Tue–Sat). It is also the Centre for Health and Healing, and multifarious groups – from the William Blake Society to the Zen Group – hold frequent meetings and lectures. St James's is also famous as a refuge. There is a caravan permanently situated in the churchyard where trained volunteers provide counselling for anybody in need of a sympathetic and confidential ear.

Just a few doors down towards Piccadilly Circus, refuge between the covers of a book can be found at what is arguably the best branch of the **Waterstone's** bookstore chain (203–206 Piccadilly). It has a bar and café on the 5th floor where you can enjoy international beers, European food and a cool view over South London.

Across the road is **Burlington Arcade**, the beautiful Victorian covered shopping street full of chic and interesting stores that are still policed by the quaintly uniformed Beadles.

St James's Church, 197 Piccadilly; tel: 020 7734 4511; www.st-james-piccadilly.org; map E3

Map Labels

100 Club • Hakkasan
Oxford Street
TOTTENHAM COURT ROAD
Centrep
Soho Square
Market Pl.
Oxford Street
Sutton Row
Oxford Circus
OXFORD CIRCUS
Photographers' Gallery
Vasco & Piero
Noel
Berwick
Wardour
Great Chapel Street
Dean Street
Soho Theatre
Greek Street
Frith Street
Foyles
Hazlitts Hotel
Phoenix Theatre
Palladium Theatre
Ping Pong
Liberty
Carlisle Street
St Annes' Court
Sheraton Street
D'Arblay
Princi
The Soho
Flat White
Busaba Eathai
Hummus Bros
Spiga
Bateman Street
Dog & Duck
Prince Edward Theatre
Bar Italia
The Coach & Horses
Cambi
The
Great Marlborough St
Foubert's
Masala Zone
Milk & Honey
Berwick St Market
Broadwick Street
Beak Street
Kingly St
Carnaby St
Newburgh Street
Marshall Street
Fernandez & Wells
Ramen Seto
Hamley's
Polpo
Lexington Street
Great Pulteney Street
Bridle Lane
Peter St
Yalla Yalla
Lina Stores
I. Camisa
St Anne's
Brewer St
Old Compton
Romilly St
The French House
Leong's Legends
Haozhan
Rasa Saya
CHINATOWN
Bocca di Lupo
Little Lamb
Plum Valley
Gerrard
Lisle Street
Conduit St
Regent Street
New Burlington Place
Savile Row
Golden Square
Warwick Street
Lower James St
Upper James St
Lower John St
Upper John St
Sherwood Street
Windmill St
Archer St
Rupert Street
Wardour Street
Leicester Place
Leicester Street
Leices Squa
Hix
Denman St
Trocadero Centre
Glasshouse Street
Regent Street
PICCADILLY CIRCUS
Piccadilly Circus
Coventry Street
Oxendon St
St Martin's
Sackville St
Eros
Piccadilly
Jermyn Street
Regent Street
St Alban's Street
Orange
Haymarket
Whitcomb
Panton
Britain & London Visitor Centre

SOHO

Index

1 Aldwych Hotel **H4**	Gerrard Street **D3**
100 Club **C5**	Hakkasan **D5**
Aldwych Theatre **H4**	Hamley's **A4**
Baozi Inn **E3**	Haozhan **D4**
Bar Italia **D4**	Hazlitt's Hotel **D5**
Berwick Street Market **C4**	Henry Pordes **E4**
Bocca di Lupo **C3**	Hix **B3**
Boxfresh **E4**	Hummus Bros **C4**
Bridge of Aspiration **F4**	I. Camisa **C4**
Busaba Eathai **C4**	Koenig Books **E4**
Cambridge Circus **D4**	Koh Samui **E4**
Centrepoint **D5**	Leicester Square **D3**
Coco de Mer **E5**	Leong's Legends **D4**
Courtauld Institute **H3**	Liberty **A4**
Covent Garden Hotel **E5**	Lina Stores **C4**
Covent Garden Market **F4**	Little Lamb **D3**
Donmar Warehouse **F4**	London Coliseum **E3**
Fernandez & Wells **B4**	London Transport Museum **G4**
Fifi Wilson **E4**	Masala Zone **B4**
Flat White **C4**	Milk & Honey **B4**
Foyles Books **D5**	Neal's Yard **E5**
Francis Edwards/Quinto **E4**	Nicole Farhi **F4**
Freemasons' Hall **G5**	Palace Theatre **D4**

Paul Smith **F4**	Spiga **C4**
Photographers' Gallery **B5**	St Anne's **D4**
Piccadilly Circus **C3**	St Martin's Lane Hotel **E3**
Ping Pong **B4**	St Paul **F3**
Plum Valley **D3**	Stephen Jones Millinery **G5**
Polpo **B4**	Superdry **E4**
Prince Edward Theatre **D4**	Ted Baker **F4**
Princi **C4**	The Coach & Horses **D4**
Ramen Seto **A4**	The Dog & Duck **D4**
Rasa Sayang **D4**	The French House **D4**
Rock & Sole Plaice **F5**	The Ivy **E4**
Royal Opera House **G4**	The Savoy **G3**
Rules **F3**	The Soho Hotel **C4**
Seven Dials **E4**	Vasco & Piero **B5**
Simpson's-in-the-Strand **G3**	Wahaca **F3**
Soho Theatre **C5**	Waterloo Bridge **H2**
Somerset House **H3**	Yalla Yalla **C4**

46 © A-Z/OS

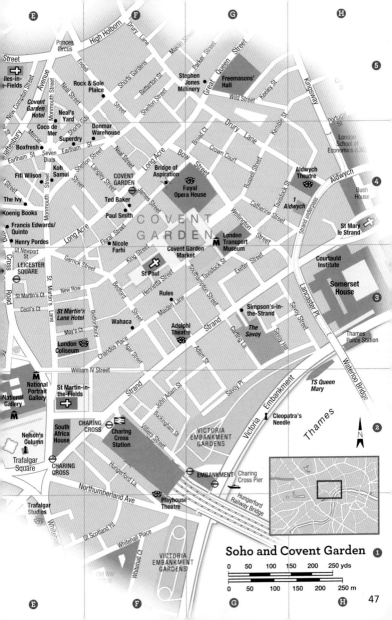

Soho and Covent Garden

| 0 | 50 | 100 | 150 | 200 | 250 yds |
| 0 | 50 | 100 | 150 | 200 | 250 m |

Enjoy **Italian delicacies** and *ambiente* in and around **Bar Italia** on Frith Street

Soho was traditionally London's French quarter and the Italians were to the east in Clerkenwell, but due to road building and slum clearances at the outbreak of World War I, they started drifting west towards Soho, and by 1934 it was regarded as more Italian than French. Soho is constantly updating itself, but many names from those days are still cheerfully dishing up pasta and pie with typical Latin flair to this day, including the celebrated **Vasco and Piero's Pavilion** (15 Poland St; tel: 020 7437 8774; map B5), a packed and bustling place with friendly service and lovely classic dishes from Umbria.

And two wonderful Italian delicatessens have survived all the renovations – **I. Camisa** (61 Old Compton St; map C4) which is small and crowded but bursting with great meats and cheeses and olives, perfect for an impromptu picnic in any quiet little enclave such as **Soho Square** a block to the north or **St Anne's** churchyard on Wardour Street – and **Lina Stores** (18 Brewer Street; map C4) which hasn't changed decor since the 1930s and has a wide variety of delicious home-baked goods.

Any self-respecting tour of Soho, however, should start, and finish, at the 24-hour café, **Bar Italia** (22 Frith Street; tel: 020

7437 4520; map D4). In honesty, it might not have the best espresso, but what it does have in spades is authentic Italian atmosphere and style. It also provides excellent people-watching from its small terrace. And if you choose to go on a night that the Italian football team is playing you will find it at its most characteristically colourful and noisy as fans cram into the small back room to watch the game on the big screen.

Next door (21) is its posher sister restaurant, **Little Italy** (tel: 020 7287 3514), which is a little pricey but has very good, deceptively simple Italian food, is favoured by Brit celebs and

frequently clears the floor for dancing after dinner.

Princi (135 Wardour Street; map C4) is the London outpost of Milan's bakery and coffee house. And it has a similarly fashion-conscious crowd. It's a very smart marble-countered place, where the beautiful people gather post-work or pre-club, for coffee and pastries or a glass of wine and a couple of shared *crostini* or a more substantial savoury snack. **Polpo** (41 Beak St; map B4) is a bustling, Venetian *bacaro* bar with lots of delicious tapas-sized portions of *cichetti*, *crostini* and *pizzettas*.

Spiga (84–86 Wardour St; tel: 020 7734 3444; map C4) has tasty stone-fired thin-crust pizzas many would name as the best in London. Be sure to ask for a booth when being seated as the free-standing tables jostle a little too closely for comfort.

The lavishly praised **Bocca di Lupo** (12 Archer St; tel: 020 7734 2223; map C3) is a buzzy, lively place where the walls are hung with paintings by the chef's mother. And the menu has gathered together all the brilliant regional dishes – soups, pastas, risottos and roasts – of Italy into one enticing list.

Set off on a mini pub crawl of **characterful Soho pubs** starting at the French House

The French House (49 Dean St; map D4) once had a proper pub's name, but it became so widely known as 'The French' (rumours abound that it was the meeting place for the French Resistance in London during World War II) that the owners gave in and had a sign made up naming it officially. The drinking den of the poet Dylan Thomas and the painter Francis Bacon, The French still gets its fair share of bohos and old reprobates. Rather eccentrically, they only serve beer by the half pint, but the selection of wines is magnifique!

The Coach & Horses (29 Greek St; map D4) is much-favoured by writers and media types. This is partly due to the legend of Jeffrey Bernard, a journalist best known for his *Low Life* column in the

Spectator, whose dedication to drink often rendered him unable to work, so the words 'Jeffrey Bernard is Unwell' would appear in place of his column: words that inspired a book and a play about him. Have a vodka and tonic, Bernard's favourite tipple, in his honour.

The Dog & Duck (18 Bateman St; map D4) is an attractive Victorian pub – there was a time you could shoot snipe in Leicester Fields, now Leicester Square, hence the name. If packed, and it often is, head upstairs to the George Orwell Room (he used to celebrate the launch of his books here) where you are more likely to get a seat. Ale-tasting sessions are held here on Mondays.

If you have had your fill of pubs but not of drinking, go to **Milk & Honey** (61 Poland St; map B4) a laid-back bar with great, and reasonable for central London, cocktails. It is a members-only club, but open to all-comers on certain days; check their website (www.mlkhny.com/london).

Another cool bar to end your tour is **Mark's Bar**, the basement bar beneath the acclaimed restaurant **Hix Soho** (66 Brewer St; tel: 020 7292 3518; map B3), which has comfortable Chesterfield sofas and a great clubby feel.

Glory in the mock-Tudor splendour of **Liberty**, London's most **distinctive department store**

Liberty has always been strongly associated with the Arts and Crafts and Art Nouveau movements and continues to showcase new designers to this day, whether it is cutting-edge fashion by Christopher Kane, furniture by Vitra, or more routine items, such as bags, books, bikinis or bracelets. The basement has a beautifully laid-out menswear department. There is also a stylish café, as strong on people-watching as it is for tea and cake (and, incidentally, there are also some very chic and clean bathrooms). The ground floor has beauty, jewellery (lots of lovely Art Deco pieces), accessories and the sumptuous haven of the scarf hall where you can find traditional Liberty prints such as the famous ostrich-feather pattern alongside pieces by up-and-coming talents. Upstairs in the wood-pannelled galleried rooms you can find Liberty's very eclectic selection of womenswear.

Liberty, 214-220 Regent Street; tel: 020 7734 2134; map A4

NEWBURGH STREET

Time was, Carnaby Street typified 'Swinging London', but those days are long gone and it is now lined with outlets for global brands. The real design action can now be found one small block behind in Newburgh Street (map B4). Check out: **Beyond the Valley** (2) for fashion-forward clothes and accessories; **Blaqua** (9) for sharp '60s inspired menswear; **Beatrix Ong** (8) for elegant women's shoes; **Peckham Rye** (11) for rakish '40s-inspired menswear; **Twenty8twelve** (13) for sophisticated women's clothing designed by Sienna Miller's sister Savannah; **Onitsuka Tiger** (15) for sneaker obsessives; **Chateau Roux** (17) for '80s-influenced clothes galore.

Eat your way round the world in and around Wardour Street

Hummus Bros (88 Wardour St; tel: 020 7734 1311; map C4) really know how to make a meal out of hummus. They send it out with plenty of hot pitta bread, pile on delicious toppings such as chicken and guacamole or slow-cooked beef with caramelised onions, and offer lovely Mediterranean salads and side dishes to accompany. **Busaba Eathai** (106–110 Wardour St; tel: 020 7255 8686; map C4) always seems to have a long queue outside, but is worth a wait for the flavour-packed Thai specials. **Masala Zone** (9 Marshall St; tel: 020 7287 9966; map B4) is a mini chain but don't hold that against it – it has absolutely delicious, reasonably priced Indian street foods. The lunch-only *pau bhaji*,

or Bombay sandwich – a pile of chilli-hot grilled vegetables in naan bread – is a revelation. **Ping Pong** (45 Great Marlborough St; tel: 020 7851 6969; map B4) is another restaurant you'd never guess was part of a chain, albeit a small and select one. They specialise in Chinese dumplings – it's dim sum without the hoopla.

Yalla Yalla (1 Greens Court; tel: 020 7287 7663; map C4) is a small hip café serving Beirut street food. **Rasa Sayang** (5 Macclesfield St; tel: 020 7734 1382; D4) has delicious one-dish meals from Malaysia and Singapore, most of which are well under a tenner. **Ramen Seto** (19 Kingly St; tel: 020 7434 0309; map A4) is a home from home for London's Japanese community, and the queue for takeaway at lunch time shows just how popular it is with the area's office workers. Set meals are excellent value.

If you want a coffee after, or were only ever interested in the caffeine course, proceed directly to **Fernandez & Wells** (73 Beak St; map B4) for what is widely talked of as the best coffee in London. **Flat White** (17 Berwick St; map C4) is another good spot for coffee that makes it the way the Antipodeans like it.

Have a night at the **Royal Opera House**

There's more to the Royal Opera House than meets the eye. It's not just a world-class opera house, it is also home to The Royal Ballet and The Linbury Studio Theatre, where experimental dance and music are staged. Built in 1732, the four-tiered main auditorium was regilded and restored to former glory in 1999 – a suitably grand setting for world-famous tenors, divas and celebrated ballerinas – and in an active attempt to rope in the masses a range of cheap tickets is offered for all performances. Even if classical entertainments are not your cup of tea, the 2.5-acre Opera House merits a visit. The centrepiece of the renovation is a soaring arched-glass atrium, and the **Amphitheatre Restaurant** on the top floor is a spacey minimalist setting for light lunches and pre-opera meals. In warmer months grab a seat on its outdoor terrace which has fantastic views across Covent Garden Piazza.

The only way to truly appreciate how vast the Royal Opera House is, is to take a tour (10.30am, 12.30pm and 2.30pm Mon–Fri, every half hour on Sat). Visitors are led up and down all eight floors and are afforded a good old nosey around the workshops that produce the scores of costumes required for each production. On the morning tours you can see the ballerinas in rehearsal.

Royal Opera House, Bow Street; tel: 020 7304 4000; www.roh.org.uk; map G4

See how British design guru Sir **Paul Smith** has turned **Floral Street** into menswear central

When Paul Smith bought his first shop – a dilapidated former bakery – on **Floral Street** in 1975, the entire area was a wasteland. The fruit and vegetable market had been closed down and its transformation into the Piazza shopping centre and tourist attraction wasn't completed until 1980. So when the first London Paul Smith store opened fashion hounds had to make a pilgrimage into Covent Garden for his 'classic with a twist' take on British menswear and eclectic collection of other objects and curiosities for sale. The original shop has expanded, and where Sir Paul (he was knighted in 2000) led, others have followed, making Floral Street an ideal location to browse menswear outfitters.

The **Paul Smith** emporium (40–44 Floral St) is four connected shops you can wander around, with men's and women's collections of dapper essentially English, but not at all stuffy clothing, plus lots of accessories and trinkets in his signature stripes. Next door at no 39 is his dedicated shoe store. Across the road is hip, streetwear label, **Maharishi** (19) with its variations on cargo and camouflage, and one of the rising names in British menswear, **Nigel Hall** (15 and 18), who is known for his sharply cut casual and smart-casual clothes. French designer **Agnes B** (35) has her understated, beautifully cut men's suits and leisure wear in the basement and on the ground floors. **Nicole Farhi** (11) has her dedicated menswear store here (womenswear is at 4 The Piazza). Or there's **Jack Wills** (34) for the British take on preppy. And **Ted Baker** (9–10) for mid-price, good-quality, high-street fashion.

Don't forget to look up when in Floral Street or you'll miss the 'Bridge of Aspiration', the ethereal glass and aluminium walkway that provides the dancers of the Royal Ballet School with a direct link to the Royal Opera House.

Floral Street; map F4

Sample **dim sum, dumplings and duck** in London's small but perfectly formed **Chinatown**

London's Chinatown may be small but what it lacks in size it makes up in colour and character. Also, it is on the doorstep of London's theatreland which, with its swiftly served, inexpensive food available all day and on into the small hours, makes it very convenient as part of a night out in the West End. In recent years some exciting restaurants have moved in to shake up the scene, and create a gastro buzz. The most notable are:

Haozhan (8 Gerrard St; tel: 020 7434 3838; map D4) has food from all over China as well as delightful European-influenced oddities such as Marmite prawns and coffee pork ribs. **Plum Valley** (20 Gerrard St; tel: 020 7494 4366; map D3) has excellent and adventurous dim sum at lunchtime, and a range of rice dishes cooked in a clay

pot as an evening meal for two. **Leong's Legends** (4 Macclesfield St; tel: 020 7287 0288; map D4) is highly praised for its excellent spicy and garlicky Taiwanese food, though the service can be brusque. The atmospheric **Baozi Inn** (25 Newport Court; tel: 020 287 6877; map E3) is named after the savoury stuffed bun that is the ubiquitous snack of northern China; their version is top-notch, as is the rest of the Chengdu street food. **Little Lamb** (72 Shaftesbury Avenue; tel: 020 7287 8078; map D3), an outpost of a mainland China chain, serves the best Mongolian hot pot. The title for London's best Chinese restaurant, however, most frequently goes to **Hakkasan** (8 Hanway Place; tel: 020 7907 1888, map D5), a sleek, sexy, very 'in' basement restaurant.

Take a seat at one of theatreland's most exciting 'little' theatres, the **Donmar Warehouse**

You can't judge a book by its cover and you perhaps shouldn't be able to judge a play by its theatre. And yet, chances are if you pick a play, any play, put on by the Donmar Warehouse, you will have picked a winner. It is only little – it seats 250 – but it is easily the most influential theatre in London, having staged productions that have gone on to receive 35 Olivier Awards (British theatre awards) and 14 Tony Awards (for Broadway productions) between them. Founded in the 1960s, down a cobbled street in a warehouse once used for ripening bananas, the Donmar housed the Royal Shakespeare Company in the '70s, and all Britain's most innovative touring companies in the '80s. Then in 1992 Sam Mendes took over as artistic director and began season after season of attention-getting theatre, much of which went on to transfer to the West End and Broadway. In 2002 Mendes left to become the renowned film director of *American Beauty* and *Revolutionary Road* and Michael Grandage took over. Amazingly, the Donmar's record for churning out award-winning productions – which have included *Frost/Nixon*, Jude Law's *Hamlet*, *Parade* and *Piaf* to name but a few – has not

faltered. Tickets are hard to come by, but worth planning ahead for. It's not the most comfortable theatre – the 'seats' are upholstered benches and not exactly roomy – but somehow its rough edges and limited size add to the intensity.

Donmar Warehouse, 41 Earlham St; tel: 0844 871 7624; www.donmarwarehouse. com; map F4

PICK OF THE FRINGE

The Donmar Warehouse, the **Royal Court** *(p.56)*, the **Young Vic** *(p.136)*, the **Almeida** *(p.162)* and the **Tricycle** in Kilburn *(www.tricycle.co.uk)* are the main outlets for new writing, which between them have pioneered many of London's most exciting recent productions. Lively pub theatres include the **King's Head** in Islington *(p.162)*, the **Gate** in Notting Hill *(www.gatetheatre.co.uk)* and the **Bush Theatre** in Shepherd's Bush *(www.bushtheatre.co.uk)*.

Hunt for **vintage editions** or a cheap paperback in this well-loved **bookshop-lined street**

Whether you crave a rare first edition or the latest bestseller, **Charing Cross Road** is well worth a browse. **Foyles** (113–119) is not only the largest bookshop on the street, it's the largest in Europe, with five floors, and more than 200,000 titles, and each of the 20-plus departments is overseen by an expert. The whole place has a charming but slightly chaotic feel. They also stock records and sheet music and have frequent signings, exhibitions and other events including literary lunches and dinners (www.foyles.co.uk for details). **Ray's Jazz Café** on the first floor is very boho and has lovely big windows looking out over Charing Cross Road.

If design books are in your plan, try **Koenig Books** (80), an inspiring shop specialising in art, architecture and photography. **Francis Edwards** (72) is an antiquarian bookseller dealing in all subjects but particularly strong on military, travel and art. In the basement is secondhand bookshop **Quinto** (72), known for its 'changeovers' on the first Tuesday of every month, when you often see queues of eager readers outside. All the old stock is dispatched to the mother shop in Hay on Wye (the small Welsh town that hosts a happening annual literary festival) and all the new books freshly placed on the shelves. **Henry Pordes** (58–60) has leatherbound first editions among the more accessible finds, and the informed staff are only too happy to debate the relative merits of any book with you. The one place you won't find a bookshop is at no. 84 where Marks & Co, the inspiration for the book, and later film, *84 Charing Cross Road*, once stood. It is now the pub chain, All Bar One, and not recommended.

Charing Cross Rd; map D5–E3

Enjoy the **cultural riches** and open-air entertainments of **Somerset House**

Thanks to an ambitious refurbishment that began in 1997, Somerset House remains one of England's finest 18th-century buildings with its courtly square, 55 fountains, beautiful old gaslights and spacious terrace giving out on to the Thames. Former headquarters of the Inland Revenue, Somerset House now encompasses a university, a fine art museum, several restaurants and cafés, and an educational centre running workshops for adults and activities for children. Plus there's an exciting programme of open-air films and concerts in the summer (June and July), and an ice rink in the winter

(November to January). It is truly a house for all moods and seasons. Perhaps the best way to start to explore it is with a free tour. They take 45 minutes and are at 1.15 and 2.45pm on Thursdays and 12.15, 1.15, 2.15 and 3.15pm on Saturday.

The Courtauld Gallery in the North Building houses one of the world's finest private collections of European art from the Renaissance to the 20th century, best known for its fine collection of Impressionist and Post-Impressionist paintings including many famous ones by Monet, Manet, Van Gogh (including his *Self Portrait* pictured left), Gauguin, Degas and Cézanne. And there are a handful of more modern works by Modigliani, Matisse and Kandinsky.

The Admiralty restaurant has a nautical, old gentlemen's club theme as a nod to the naval officers based here long ago. The food is modern and European and the room fills up with happy chatter at lunch times. **The River Terrace** is a more formal, more expensive French restaurant, but on a warm evening there is no finer place to sit out and watch the world float by.

Somerset House, Strand; tel: 020 7836 7613; www.somersethouse.org.uk; map H3

Rock out at the **100 Club** and down London's
Tin Pan Alley

The history of the **100 Club** (100 Oxford St; tel: 020 7636 0933; map C5) spans 50 years, but it is most famous for two nights in September 1976 when it hosted the world's first Punk Festival. The Sex Pistols, The Clash, The Damned, Siouxsie & the Banshees, and the Buzzcocks took the stage. No one had heard of any of them, and not one of them had a record deal. But they soon did. Those now legendary nights changed the club's image (it had been a down-at-heel jazz venue until then) and its fortunes. Many high-profile bands have since appeared here – The Rolling Stones (*pictured*) played a secret gig in 1982. It went on to have another flowering in the indie years of the 1990s when it put on Oasis and The White Stripes among others. It is now best known for its Northern Soul all-nighters on Saturdays (go to www.the100club.co.uk for listings).

Those interested in London's rock history should walk round the corner to **Denmark Street** (map D5). London's Tin Pan Alley in the 1920s, it is still filled with specialist music shops. The Beatles, Jimi Hendrix and Stevie Wonder all recorded in the **Regents Sounds Studio** (4). Bob Marley bought his first electric guitar at **BJ & Byrne** (20) and Elton John wrote his first hit *Your Song* on their rooftop in 1970. The Sex Pistols used to live in the flat above **Hank's Guitar Shop** (6), and David Bowie is said to have spent a few months sleeping in a van outside the **Giaconda Café** (9) where he'd meet his band for egg and chips before gigs. The old café has been reborn as the very hip **Giaconda Dining Room** (9; tel: 020 7240 3334).

Dine with the establishment in the **renowned traditional restaurants** of Covent Garden

Thanks to its central location, Covent Garden has been London's first port of call for gourmands for three centuries. Between them, the following establishments have hosted most of the crowned heads of Europe and the most celebrated people of their day.

Rules (35 Maiden Lane; tel: 020 7836 5314; map F3) opened in 1798 and claims to be London's oldest restaurant. It sources all its game from its own estate in the High Pennines. While highly traditional, Rules has avoided becoming a museum piece. The food has the occasional lighter, modern touch, though puddings have remained thoroughly British with their suets and possets intact. The dining room is beautifully atmospheric.

Simpson's-in-the-Strand (100 The Strand; tel: 020 7836 9112; map G3) is as much an institution as it is a restaurant. The 'bill of fare' includes roast sirloin of beef that comes on a trolley under a huge silver dome and is carved just for you by one of an army of attentive waiters. **The Savoy Grill** (The Savoy Hotel, The Strand, map G3) was *the* place the establishment lunched. Churchill sat at table 4 every day, war and other commitments permitting. At the time of going to press The Savoy was closed for refurbishment, but was scheduled to reopen in 2010 under the management of Gordon F-word Ramsay.

The Ivy (1 West St; tel: 020 7836 4751; map E4) is theatreland's favourite dining establishment and a real celeb-magnet. One restaurant critic famously quipped: 'A table at The Ivy is one of the most sought-after pieces of furniture in London'. The classics – Caesar salad, steak tartare and fish cakes – have near legendary status, but you have to book as far as a month in advance.

For a complete contrast, one of Covent Garden's best casual, modern spots is the vibrant **Wahaca** (66 Chandos Place; tel: 020 7240 1883; map F3) for Mexican street food and cocktails in trendy buzzy surroundings.

Get to know an open secret at the **Freemasons' Hall**

Anybody who knows anything about the freemasons will know that it is a closed and very secretive society. And yet... they have left the door open to the public at their London HQ. The grand lodge was first built in 1775, as the city headquarters for what was then an occult order of men who believed that they had inherited a body of secret knowledge from before the Flood. That first building was deemed unsafe and the current hall, considered by many to be the finest Art Deco building in the country, was erected in 1932. And you are free to walk on in and get to know the freemasons of today through their library and museum, and without the use of winks, nods or funny handshakes. There are free tours of this extraordinary building on the hour every hour from 11am to 4pm on weekdays. It is worth it to see the Grand Temple alone; the massive, bronze doors open slowly out to reveal an enormous jade and marble chamber that can seat 1,700 and is magnificently, and mysteriously, decorated with the symbols and figures of Masonic ritual on panels of mosaic and stained glass.

On the same street (and named after it), **Great Queen Street** (32) is a noisy and bustling gastro-pub, offering great modern British food with a young, buzzy basement bar, **The Dive**. Another noteworthy address on the street is **Stephen Jones Millinery** (36) which sells beautiful and eccentric hats.

Freemasons' Hall, 60 Great Queen St; tel: 020 7831 9811; www.ugle.org.uk; map G5

Find tranquillity and **all things organic** in **Neal's Yard**

Just behind the commercial madness of Covent Garden, Neal's Yard is a small quiet corner offering tranquillity on many levels. Benches and seats are scattered among brightly painted oil drums filled with unusual trees and plants. There are cafés upstairs and down, offering restorative cups of tea. And treatment rooms offer shiatsu, reflexology, a dose of Chinese herbal medicine, or a bottle of lavender oil to soothe your senses. When Nicholas Saunders, a '70s hippy, opened his wholefood shop here, Neal's Yard wasn't even marked on the map, it was a rat-infested, squalid dump.

But his shop was so successful that it led to a raft of world-renowned businesses including **Neal's Yard Remedies**, the organic beauty range, and **Neal's Yard Dairy** (17 Short Gardens), specialising in the then-uncelebrated British farm cheeses. **The Neal's Yard Therapy Rooms** (tel: 020 7379 7662) are an oasis of calm which you can use as a day spa or just book in for one treatment such as a facial or massage. Tortillas, Turkish meze and tandooris are among the delicious meat-free offerings from **World Food Café**.

Neal's Yard; map E5

SEVEN DIALS

Neal's Yard is in the **Seven Dials** (www.sevendials.co.uk; map E4) area of Covent Garden, one of the hippest 'hidden villages' of the metropolis. Here you can find: **Coco de Mer** (23 Monmouth St), a sexy store concentrating on 'bedroom products' and all things sensual; **Fifi Wilson** (38 Monmouth St), a designer boutique with a quirky vintage feel; **Koh Samui** (65 Monmouth St), one of the best-loved independent boutiques for up-and-coming young labels; **Boxfresh** (2 Shorts Gardens) for bright funky urban wear for men; **Superdry** (Thomas Neal's Centre), the super-trendy young brand favoured by Kate Moss and Jude Law.

Check out what's in focus now at the
Photographers' Gallery

The Photographers' Gallery doesn't merely show emerging young photography talent, it fosters and encourages it with sponsorships, educational programmes and prizes. And also just by being there. In its 35-year history, the Gallery has played an important role in establishing photography as a serious art form in the UK. And you cannot walk into this small gallery without learning to love photography a little bit more. To look at any one of their exhibitions is to become somewhat involved in the photographers' world – to see things their way a little bit.

The gallery has a reputation for exhibiting and selling the best of international photography of all genres – news, fashion, portraiture, art and the more experimental. And they have a series of afternoon lectures that either expand on current exhibitions or explore their archives. There's also a first-floor **café** with good coffee and cake and a small selection of sandwiches and salads for lunch. The **bookshop**, however, is the real hub. It has an extensive range of photography books including many rare or limited-edition ones, and also sells Lomo cameras and some secondhand photography equipment. The staff are informed and, mostly, prepared to help you find exactly what you want, and the customers are a cool crowd who seem as much interested in hooking up with each other as they do in making purchases.

Photographers' Gallery, 16–18 Ramillies St; tel: 0845 262 1618; www.photonet.org. uk; map B5

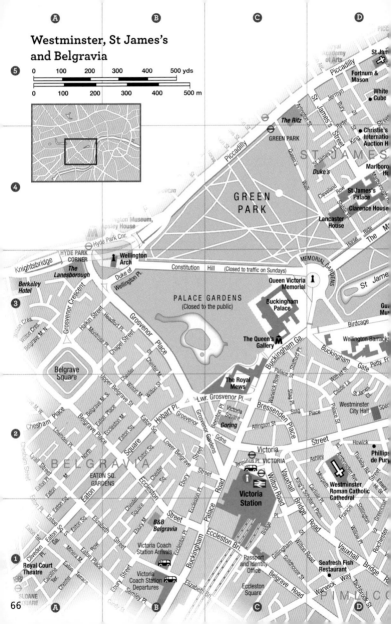

Westminster, St James's and Belgravia

0   100   200   300   400   500 yds

0   100   200   300   400   500 m

PICC

Royal Academy of Arts

St Jam

Fortnum & Mason

White Cube

Piccadilly

The Ritz

GREEN PARK

Jermyn Street

St James's Street

Bury St

Ryder St

King St

Christie's Internatio Auction H

ST JAMES

Duke's

Marlboro H

GREEN PARK

Queen's Walk

Cleveland Row

St James's Palace

Clarence House

Lancaster House

MEMORIAL GARDENS

St Jame

HYDE PARK CORNER

Wellington Arch

Knightsbridge

The Lanesborough

Berkeley Hotel

Hyde Park Cnr.

Duke of Wellington Pl.

Constitution Hill (Closed to traffic on Sundays)

Queen Victoria Memorial

PALACE GARDENS (Closed to the public)

Grosvenor Crescent

Grosvenor Place

Buckingham Palace

Gua Mu

Wilton Cres

Belgrave M. N.

Halkin Street

Headfort Pl.

Montrose Pl.

Chapel Street

St.

Wilton St.

The Queen's Gallery

Buckingham Ga

Birdcage

Wellington Barracks

Buckingham

Gate

Petty Fr

Wiltof St.

Castle La.

St James's

Belgrave Square

Upper Belgrave St.

The Royal Mews

Palace Street

Stafford Pl.

Stag Pl.

Place

Westminster City Hall

Spe

Chesham Place

Lowndes Pl.

Belgrave Place

Eaton Pl.

Wilton

Square

Wilton Pl.

Grosvenor Pl.

Beeston Pl.

Lwr. Grosvenor Pl.

Bressenden

Warwick Row

Place

Victoria Square

Goring

Affington St.

Street

Howick

Phillips de Pury

BELGRAVIA

Lyall Street

Lowndes Pl.

Eaton Square

Eaton Place

North

Eaton M.

Eaton Sq.

Lower Belgrave St.

Grosvenor Gdns

Victoria

Ashley

Terminus Pl.

VICTORIA

Vauxhall Bridge Road

King's Scholars' Pass.

Westminster Roman Catholic Cathedral

Chesham Street

Eaton Pl.

EATON SQ. GARDENS

Eaton St.

Elizabeth St.

Eccleston St.

Ebury Street

Eccleston Street

Palace Street

Victoria Station

Wilton Rd

Victoria Station

Ambrosden Ave

Thirleby Rd

Morpeth Tce

Francis

Stillington

Greycoat

Clivedon

Minera M.

Roy

Eaton Square

Eccleston Bn.

Elizabeth St.

Seafresh Fish Restaurant

Vauxhall

Royal Court Theatre

Caroline Terrace

Chester

B&B Belgravia

Victoria Coach Station Arrivals

Ebury

Buckingham Palace Road

Passport and Identity Office

Gillingham

Guildhouse St.

Belgrave Road

Warwick

Way

Tachbrook St.

Bridge

Rochester

SLOANE SQUARE

Cundy St.

Victoria Coach Station Departures

Semley Pl.

Eccleston Bn.

Eccleston Square

PIMLIC

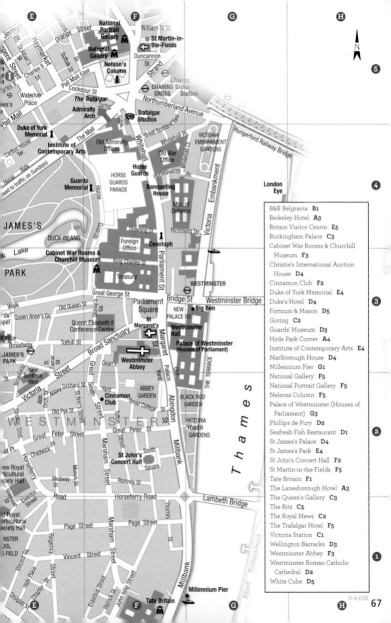

© A-Z/OS

Have a late night at **the National Gallery**

Friday Lates are a fun, cultural way to start any weekend in London. The National Gallery stays open until 9pm every Friday and you can wander about at will or stop and listen to live music, attend a lecture, join a 'walk and draw' group, have a drink at the bar or a bite in the café. The **National Café** is a good place to sit and plot your route (with more than 2,300 works in the collection, you'd do well to streamline your visit). The more formal **National Dining Rooms** is excellent for chewing over what you've seen.

The modern Sainsbury Wing contains the earliest works – mostly Italian paintings by old masters such as Giotto and Piero della Francesca. In the West Wing are Italian Renaissance masterpieces by Correggio, Titian and Raphael, and the North Wing has the 17th-century Dutch, Flemish, Italian and Spanish old masters. The gallery's most popular paintings are in the East Wing. These are largely works by the French Impressionists and post-Impressionists, including one of Monet's water-lily paintings and one of Van Gogh's sunflowers.

If you have kids in tow, there are fantastic family activities at the weekends including the magic carpet story-telling sessions in front of a selected (usually animal-filled) painting for under-5s, and painting, pottery or sculpture workshops for older children.

National Gallery, Trafalgar Square; tel: 020 7747 2885; www.nationalgallery.org. uk; daily 10am–6pm, Fri until 9pm; free entrance and free guided tours; map F5

Study the many **faces of Britain** at the **National Portrait Gallery**

The original idea behind the National Portrait Gallery was to pay tribute to the nation's great men and women – all the people, celebrated or relatively unsung, who had contributed to the nation's history. And it is useful now to treat this grand old gallery as a collection of people and faces rather than of art. This somehow makes it less stuffy.

So: who are you interested in? The gallery's first purchase was the 'Chandos' portrait, widely believed to be of William Shakespeare, and it would be easy to use this as a starting point for a tour of British literary greats. Or if power is your motivator, the Portrait Gallery (as custodians of the greatest collection of Tudor portraits in the world) has a painting of a very young Elizabeth I at her coronation by an unknown artist that exudes the forces of ambition and majesty. And there are plenty more portrayals of stiff-backed royals if they are your cup of tea. These include the first double portrait of the Princes William and Harry showing them in the dress uniform of the Household Cavalry. Or if contemporary celebrity is your obsession you can find photos of soccer players and rock stars in the more recent galleries.

The **Portrait Café** in the basement is a fun place for a quick break, and **The Portrait Restaurant** on the rooftop is a fashionable foodie destination with wonderful views of Trafalgar Square, Big Ben and the Houses of Parliament. It is open for lunch every day and dinner on Thursdays and Fridays when the gallery is open until 9pm (last orders 8.30pm).

The National Portrait Gallery, St Martin's Place; tel: 020 7306 0055; www. npg.org.uk; daily 10am–6pm, Thur and Fri until 9pm; free; map F5

Hire a deckchair and admire the ducks, geese and passing civil servants in **St James's Park**

St James's Park is home to 15 species of waterfowl, including pelicans that have been here since the Russian Ambassador presented them to Charles II in 1664. They are not actually the same ones, of course, but the tradition continues and the Russian ambassador presents two to the court as and when necessary. The Park currently has five – four from Eastern Europe and the fifth from Louisiana. Feeding time (they are given 12lbs of fish a day) is at 2.30pm. There are also ducks, geese, swans, moorhen, coots and grebe who nest here. This is amazing as grebe are very shy birds and St James's is one of the most popular parks in Europe with almost six million visitors a year.

St James's is the most romantic of the Royal Parks, with its criss-crossing paths, delicate bridge and weeping willows. So it is strange to think that in medieval times this was a soggy swamp where female lepers from the nearby St James's Hospice came to feed their pigs. It was Henry VIII who bought the land and made it into a deer park, but Charles II who landscaped it and opened it to the public. Find a bench or hire a green-and-white-striped deckchair and admire the view, which takes in Buckingham Palace, Big Ben, the London Eye, and the rear view of Whitehall and 10 Downing Street. This affords some excellent people-watching as the path that borders the eastern side of St James's Park is often filled with ministers and civil servants scurrying between meetings. Bring a picnic, or there's a restaurant, **Inn the Park**, open for all-day refreshments. *Map D-E 3-4.*

Attend **a candle-lit concert** at St Martin-in-the-Fields

Built in 1724, St Martin-in-the-Fields is the oldest building on Trafalgar Square. A church has stood on this site since the 13th century when the area was fields between the cities of London and Westminster. Ever since the turn of the 20th century, St Martin-in-the-Fields has wanted to be known as 'the church with the ever-open door'. And it lives up to the promise. The doors actually open just before 8am for the morning service, but there is something here for everyone right until the doors close after the evening concert at midnight. Even when the doors are not literally open, St Martin's is reaching out in some way. It was the first London church to allow a radio broadcast on its premises in 1924, for a Christmas appeal, and still broadcasts one annually on BBC Radio 4 which raises more than £500,000 a year for people in need. Because of its position next to the South African High Commission, the church became involved in the campaign to free Nelson Mandela and in the founding of human rights charity Amnesty International, and the homeless charities Shelter and the Big Issue.

St Martin's is best enjoyed at dusk when the candles in the chandeliers are lit, and the elegant nave fills with music. It is a magical scene; and the evening recitals are of a consistently high quality. Despite its open door and all the influence that has spread round the world through them, it is music that St Martin's is really famous for. The house orchestra, the Academy of St Martin-in-the-Fields, has played an important part in the modern British revival of Baroque music. The **café in the crypt** is a nice place to stop for a coffee at any time of day or night.

St Martin-in-the-Fields, Saint Martin's Place; tel: 020 7766 1122; www.stmartin-in-the-fields.org; map F5

Tate Britain was known simply as The Tate, until the Tate Modern opened across the river to give it some serious competition. But it would be a mistake to leave the quieter, older Tate sister out of any art tour of London. Okay, so it 'only' has British art, but there is some seriously exciting, not to mention controversial, stuff here. Over the years this has included: Sarah Lucas's 2006 Christmas tree decorated with near-pornographic cherubs equipped with impressive genitalia; Martin Creed's installation, Work No. 850, saw an athlete sprint the length of the gallery every 30 seconds in 2008; and Chris Offili's retrospective, including some of his works decorated in elephant dung, in 2010. But whatever attention-grabbing

exhibition is on during your visit, it is worth making a quick tour of Tate Britain's London landscapes. These include: Turner's *The Thames Above Waterloo Bridge*, *State Britain* by Mark Wallinger, *Shelterers in the Tube* by Henry Moore, and two Constables *Kensington Gravel Pits*, and *A Bank on Hampstead Heath*.

The restaurant is notable for its eccentric mural fantasy, *The Expedition in Pursuit of Rare Meats*, by Rex Whistler, featuring English pastoral scenes, tropical jungles, Rome's ancient chariots and a few men on bikes – a rather memorable setting for a meal. And the food is pretty good too.

Tate Britain, Millbank; tel: 020 7887 8888; www.tate.org.uk; daily 10am–6pm; free; map F1

Go for a **boat trip** on the Thames from **Millbank Millennium Pier**

The Millbank Millennium Pier is the most recent central-London pier to open. And the most garlanded; a battleship-grey streamlined structure, it has won many architectural, design and engineering prizes. Due to its proximity to Tate Britain, the artist Angela Bulloch was commissioned to create a work for the pier, but she instead transformed the entire structure into an artwork, by adding a light installation, called 'Flash and Tidal'. Yellow and blue lights glow along the decks, alternating between high and low tide, while 63 programmed white lights flash on and off, changing their sequence according to the tidal cycle. Due to the dramatic changes of level at this point in the river – it can rise or fall up to 20ft depending on the tides – the pier is moored quite far out in the river. You reach it by a long angled walkway and stand waiting for your river ride in what feels like the middle of the Thames. Seagulls wheel above your head, the waves lap – you have already escaped the city's frantic rhythm and you haven't even boarded a vessel yet.

If you are here following a visit to Tate Britain, and haven't done with art yet, just hop on the Tate to Tate boat for the 18-minute journey to Bankside Pier. Or take the opportunity to see more of the city by boat and opt for a longer journey or a full city cruise. It is a great way of cramming in the sights for those who have limited time or who want to avoid traffic of the vehicular or touristy kind. More than ten companies run cruises and ferries from the pier (check the pier's website for details). You can choose between powerboat trips or more sedate cruise packages, with or without commentary, with or without lunch or dinner or drinks or entertainments.

The Millbank Millennium Pier, Millbank; www.millbankpier.co.uk; map F1–G1

The **mother of all parliaments** and a choice dinner at the **Cinnamon Club**

A tour of the **Houses of Parliament** is a fascinating experience. British visitors can tour the House throughout the year, but tours must be arranged through their member of parliament and can require as much as six months' notice. Overseas visitors may only visit during the summer recess and are accompanied by a trained guide on a tour. This takes around 75 minutes, and lets you see the debating chambers of the Commons and the Lords, and the Queen's Robing Room, where Her Majesty changes into her state robes for the annual state opening of parliament. Sadly the tours don't allow you to climb up Big Ben, arguably the world's most famous clock, but you do at least get a closer look at it.

If treading the corridors of power has given you an appetite and you feel the need to continue in the manner to which you have become accustomed, go to the **Cinnamon Club**. This is a very grand affair, filled with gossiping MPs, parliamentrary correspondents and civil servants, and is set in an old library building. The food is imaginatively rendered, richly spiced food from India. They open at 7.30am and breakfast is a particular treat.

Houses of Parliament, Parliament Square; tel: 020 7219 4206; www.parliament.uk, map G3
Cinnamon Club, 30–32 Great Smith St; tel: 020 7222 2555, map F2

Explore the **White Cube**, an ultramodern gallery, in old-world St James's

If you walk down Duke Street, with its many fine Georgian houses, and peer down a dark little alley, you'll be in for a surprise. For in the middle of Mason's Yard stands a stark grey-and-white oblong box. It looks as though it has been dropped there by aliens, but is in fact the White Cube – the gallery that is home to Lucien Freud, Chuck Close, Damien Hirst, Tracey Emin, Gilbert and George and Antony Gormley. The first White Cube opened round the corner on Duke Street in 1993 and was a small room within a room, literally a cube painted white. It soon outgrew that and moved to larger premises in Hoxton in 2002. Four years later they returned with a second gallery in Mason's Yard, the idea being that Mason's Yard focuses on leading contemporary artists while Hoxton deals with the up-and-comings. The custom-built gallery has few windows to allow maximum (white) wall space within, but is crowned by a glass lightbox. White Cube is a commercial gallery but the public is welcome and its stated purpose is to 'stage something dramatic'.

White Cube, 25–26 Mason's Yard; tel: 020 7930 5373; www.whitecube.com; Tue–Sat 10am–6pm; map D5

MORE CONTEMPORARY ART
Surprisingly for an area with such a stuffy reputation, St James's has strong links with contemporary art. Here are some other places to explore this ironic juxtapositioning.
The Institute of Contemporary Arts (12 Carlton House Terrace; tel: 020 7930 8619; www.ica.org. uk; map E4) is housed somewhat improbably in a very grand Nash building on the processional avenue, The Mall. Inside they have DJ nights in the lively bar, cinema (they are often the first London venue to show foreign art films), animation, lectures, concerts and installations from the newest movements and innovators in the world of modern art. **Phillips de Pury** (Howick Place; tel: 020 7318 4010; map D2) is an auction house that looks and acts like a contemporary art gallery. There is lots of stunning art and photography to look at and a very cool café to kick back in.

Gaze up to the most **celestial ceilings** in London at the **Banqueting House**

In a typically immodest claim, Flemish artist Peter Paul Rubens declared: 'My talent is such that no undertaking, however vast in size or diversified in subject, has ever surpassed my courage.' His courage may well have been tested by the commission to decorate the ceiling of The Banqueting House. Rubens was asked in 1634, by Charles I, to paint three massive canvases (two measuring 30 x 20ft and one of 43 x 10ft). The theme was to illustrate the wisdom and virtue of Charles's father, James I. The resulting canvases are the only ones by any important 17th-century artist that are still in position in the place they were intended for. And they are magnificent to behold – the crowning glory of this beautiful Inigo Jones building that James I had put up in 1619 as the place in which he could entertain foreign ambassadors. It was the site of splendid court balls and dinners, and remains a place of entertainment to this day, hosting corporate events, fashion shows and wedding receptions. It is still also occasionally used by the Queen for banquets; she famously entertained George Bush here in 2003, causing anti-war protestors to gather at the gates. But, while entertaining has always been its bread and butter, the Banqueting House is best known in the history books for a rather grim occasion – the execution of Charles I. He walked through a window out onto a wooden scaffold in front of it in 1649. More happily, on the ground floor is the magnificent vaulted Undercroft where Charles II had raucous drinking parties. The Banqueting House is frequently closed for events, so check for closures before planning a visit.

The Banqueting House, Whitehall; tel: 020 7930 4179; www.hrp.org.uk; Mon–Sat 10am–5pm; map F4

Feel history come to life in the **Cabinet War Rooms**, Churchill's wartime bunker

London, it's a cliché to say, is full of history. But there is nowhere quite so perfectly frozen in time as the **Cabinet War Rooms**. In 1938, with war threatening, the basement of this Whitehall building was chosen as the Cabinet War Rooms – a shelter for the heart of government and military command. Over the next six years, hundreds of men and women, civilian and uniformed, spent thousands of vital hours working – and sleeping – in this maze of interlocking, underground rooms. The slightly claustrophobic chambers and the narrow corridors leading to them are in the exact same condition they were left in when locked up at the end of hostilities in 1945. In the Map Room you can trace the position of Allied forces as they triumphed on VJ Day. The pencils are still neatly placed by the notepads on the Cabinet Room table, and the public safety posters warning 'walls have ears' or beseeching you to 'keep calm and carry on' are still pinned to the noticeboards. You can almost hear the clackety clack of the typing pool and imagine the *basso profondo* of 'Winnie' practising his speeches to rally the nation as you walk through these 30, once top-secret, rooms. Stop at the **Switch Room Café**, halfway round, for a nice pot of tea and slice of cake.

Churchill Museum & Cabinet War Rooms, Clive Steps, King Charles St; tel: 020 7930 6961; www.iwm.org.uk; daily 9.30am–6pm; map F3

Grace the royal apartments at **Buckingham Palace**

When the Queen packs her bags and goes off to her Scottish castle, Balmoral, for her summer holidays, Joe Public is invited in to her London residence to have a nose around. 'Buck House', as it is known to London's taxi drivers, has 775 rooms – including 52 bedrooms, 188 staff bedrooms, 92 offices and 78 bathrooms. Only the state rooms are open to visitors in the months of August and September. But they are the grandest of them all and do not disappoint with their glittering vistas of marble and gold leaf, walls liberally plastered with masterpieces by Rembrandt, Rubens and Canaletto, and the massive twinkling chandeliers on high. Highlights are the theatrical **Throne Room**, with the 1953 coronation throne, **The Ballroom**, where you can admire the sword the Queen uses to knight people, **The Music Room** featuring lapis lazuli columns between arched floor-to-ceiling windows, and the alabaster-and-gold plasterwork of the **White Drawing Room**.

The Queen's Gallery was built by the Queen in 1962 to allow the public year-round access to the Royal Collections – the half-million pieces of art and treasure acquired by monarchs over the past five centuries, including royal portraits by Holbein and Van Dyck, paintings by Rembrandt, Rubens and Canaletto, and drawings by Leonardo, Raphael and Michelangelo. Some pieces date back to 1498, Henry VII's reign. But George IV, who amassed most of the Dutch and Flemish masterpieces, was its most enthusiastic contributor.

The collections also flourished during the 64-year reign of Queen Victoria, but her penchant was oil paintings of family life and her favourite pets. Elizabeth II is said to have little interest in buying art, preferring to focus on conserving rather than adding to the treasures.

The first floor of the gallery has lovely views over the extent of the palace gardens, and the grand public bathrooms on the ground floor by the door are almost worth the admission price alone.

Buckingham Palace; tel: 020 7766 7300; www.royal.gov.uk. The Queen's Gallery: tel: 020 7839 1377; www.royalcollection. org.uk; daily 10am–5.30pm; map C3

Visit **Wellington Barracks**, home of the regiments who protect the Queen, and **try on a bearskin hat**

The tourists line up, sometimes ten-deep, outside the gates of Buckingham Palace to watch the changing of the guard at 11am. The Guard Mounting, as it is more properly called, actually starts at 11.30am and is quite a spectacle. But it can be an unpleasant scrum from which you cannot really get a good view. Much more sensible then to visit the guards at home in **Wellington Barracks**. If you time your visit for 10.50am (daily Apr–Aug) you will be able to see the Guards getting into formation in preparation for their march up to St James's Palace and Buckingham Palace for the changing of the Guard. Then if your interest in 'the bearskin boys' has been piqued, you could have a look around the **Guards Museum**. Inside, you will learn about the five regiments – the Grenadier Guards, Coldstream Guards, Scots Guards, Irish Guards and Welsh Guards – which, together with the Household Cavalry, the Life Guards, and the Blues and Royals, make up the Household Division of the Army charged with protecting Queen Elizabeth and Prince Philip. On display are uniforms, helmets, instruments, medals, a tent from the Crimean War and the military tunic worn

by a 16-year-old Princess Elizabeth to take the salute at the Trooping of the Colour in 1947. And if you have ever wondered what it was like to wear one of those awkward-looking tall bearskin hats, just ask and you will be permitted to try one on. It might give you renewed respect for the guards when you realise just what a trial it is to remain unsmiling under such a heavy and tickly thing.

Wellington Barracks, Birdcage Walk; tel: 020 7414 3271; www.theguards museum.com; daily 10am–4pm; map D3

Pay your respects to poets and kings in **Westminster Abbey** and be inspired by **Westminster Cathedral**

As the venue for most of the country's coronations since 1066, **Westminster Abbey** has been the backdrop to the pageant of British history. This glorious medieval church, parts of which date back to 1055, is still dedicated to the celebration of great events in the British nation. Most of the kings and queens of England are buried here and Poet's Corner has memorials to Chaucer, Shakespeare, Byron, Keats, the Brontës, Dickens – almost all the giants of British letters. The Henry VII Chapel (*pictured*) is particularly spectacular. The Abbey also has a long musical tradition, and attending Evensong, sung by the Boys' Choir of Westminster School, is a clever way to see Westminster Abbey without having to battle the crowds, as it closes to visitors an hour before Evensong begins. (Evensong is every day except Wednesday and Sunday; try to get there by 2.45pm.)

A 15-minute walk away is the less visited but no less lovely **Westminster Cathedral**. The British poet laureate, Sir John Betjeman, best known for his poems celebrating suburban life, was a devoted fan of this early Byzantine-styled Catholic cathedral. He called it a series of surprises and remarked that 'the greatest surprise of all [is] that the Cathedral looks larger inside than it looks from the outside'. Like the Abbey, Westminster Cathedral has a strong reputation for music. The Sung High Mass is an uplifting experience with incense and legions of altar servers. But most people visit Westminster Cathedral to shimmy up to the top of the bell tower – an excellent vantage point from which to view London.

Westminster Abbey; tel: 020 7222 5152; www.westminster-abbey.org; map F3
Westminster Cathedral, 42 Francis St; tel: 020 7798 9055; www.westminster cathedral.org.uk; map D2

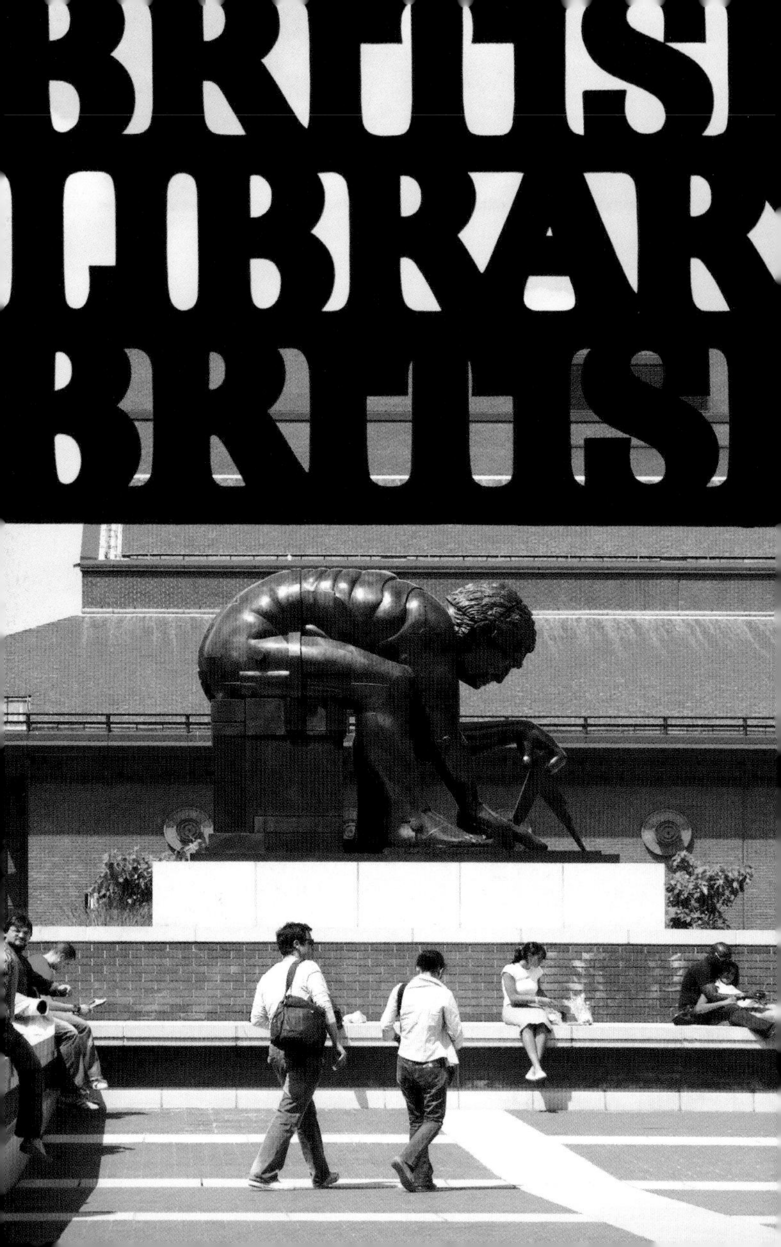

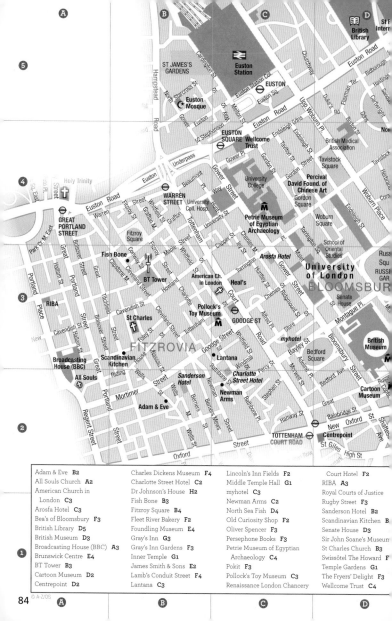

Embark on your own architectural tour using the **Royal Institute of British Architecture** as a base

It should come as no surprise that the Royal Institute of British Architecture (**RIBA**) has a beautiful building. If they couldn't knock themselves up a nice house, who could? Their headquarters is a grand 1930s building in white Portland stone with fine Art Deco carvings, and a massively impressive front door. What is a bit of surprise, however, is that as well as a world-leading architecture library, bookshop and exhibition space, RIBA has a fantastic little bar just inside the entry on the ground floor. There's also a first-floor restaurant with good food at standard London prices, so not particularly cheap, but worth considering in clement weather as it has an outdoor terrace. The café on the first-floor landing has soups, salads and sandwiches. And the lobby bar has great grilled breakfast sandwiches that are perfect to set you up for an architectural tour of your own devising or a walk around Regent's Park (a five-minute walk away at the top of Portland Place).

Within walking distance and a good focus for any architectural tour is the **BT Tower** (60 Cleveland St; map B3). Erected in 1964, it was the first purpose-built tower to transmit high-frequency radio waves. This was the time of 'Swinging London', and the tower, with its popular rotating restaurant, epitomised the exciting new scientific and architectural skills of the technical revolution. But the restaurant closed in 1980 and public access ceased . At the time of going to press, however, there was talk of finding a top British chef to reopen a restaurant on the tower's revolving platform in time for the 2012 Olympics.

RIBA, 66 Portland Place; tel: 020 7580 5533; open daily; map A3

Discover sad realities and **beautiful art** at the **Foundling Museum**

To walk around the graceful rooms of this fine Georgian building is to risk being overwhelmed by sadness along with fascination. Britain's first Foundling Hospital opened on this site in 1741 with a mission to take in abandoned or illegitimate children. When a woman left her baby here she would place a 'foundling token' with it so that, should she ever be able to come back and claim her child, they could match her to it. The tokens were carefully recorded by the hospital. Sadly most of them stayed in the hospital, and they must number among the most poignant museum artefacts it's possible to see. They might be a coin, a button, a ribbon, or a poem; as you look at them you can almost feel the desperation that led these often shabby little objects to be in the care of the hospital.

The Foundling Hospital was founded by Thomas Coram, a sea captain and philanthropist, with support from his two friends William Hogarth and George Friedrich Handel. Hogarth donated a fine portrait of Coram, and some etchings, to the hospital and encouraged his artist friends to donate works too. Thus it became Britain's first ever public art gallery with a nationally important collection that includes a Gainsborough and Joshua Reynolds. Handel donated the manuscript to his *Messiah*, and there is a room devoted to him on the top floor. It has some very comfortable red leather musical armchairs – press a button and you can hear the music he wrote for the hospital – a beautiful and restful way to end your visit.

Just opposite there's a playground, **Coram's Fields**, with fountains and a small petting zoo open to any child, but not to adults unless they are accompanied by a child.

Foundling Museum, 40 Brunswick Square; tel: 020 7841 3600; www. foundlingmuseum.org.uk; Tue-Sat 10am–5pm, Sun from 11am; children under 16 free; map E4

Scoff traditional, home-made **British fare** in a **Fitzrovia public house**

If it's a pie you are after, there's no better place to have one than **The Pie Room** at **The Newman Arms** (pictured). There are many delicious fillings to choose from, including the traditional stalwarts that are on the menu every day – steak and kidney; lamb and rosemary; chicken, gammon and leek, plus a few specials chalked on the board. They all come topped with flaky home-made pastry and accompanied by potatoes and seasonal vegetables, and will come in at under a tenner with a pint.

For a roast that cannot be rivalled, try **The Adam & Eve**. This good-looking shabby-chic gastro-pub serves classic Sunday lunches all day, or go for a rib-eye steak and chips, or on a very cold day the lamb casserole with dumplings is an excellent choice. Also bear The Adam & Eve in mind for a mid-shopping spree snack, as it is just a purse's throw from Oxford Street and has a good selection of sandwiches.

If you want to veer off the British path, **Lantana** is a little bit of Australia in Fitzrovia. The food is great – especially the breakfasts and innovative salads at lunch time – and the atmosphere crackles with Ozzie bonhomie.

The Newman Arms, 23 Rathbone St; tel: 020 7636 1127; map C2
The Adam & Eve, 77a Wells St; tel: 020 7636 0717; map B2
Lantana, 13 Charlotte Place; tel: 020 7637 3347; map C3

Feel the massed power of **14 million books** in the reading rooms of the **British Library**

There was a great deal of tutting among literary types when the British Library left its beautiful setting in the British Museum for a custom-built site near King's Cross. But even the most die-hard critics of the plain red-brick exterior cannot fail to be charmed by the bright accommodating interior. There are five floors beneath the ground and nine above, and the corridors and open spaces are all dotted with chairs complete with bookrest, lamp and plug to charge your laptop. These are not only convenient for study but also for some of the best people-watching in the city. Academics, writers and book-lovers from all over the world come here and they make interesting viewing (anyone can visit the building, but to use the reading rooms you need to apply for a Reader's Pass; see the website for details).

The not-so-studious can linger at the forecourt's **Last Word Café** with views of Eduardo Paolozzi's imposing bronze of Isaac Newton, or at the first-floor lunch rooms which have a nice open-air terrace.

The most spectacular of the reading rooms is Humanities, constructed on three levels with daylight filtered through the ceiling. In the **Sir John Ritblat Gallery** you can see some of the greatest treasures of the written word, including the much-scribbled-on drafts of works by James Joyce, a 14th-century manuscript of 'Sir Gawain and the Green Knight' (one of the first illustrated works in the English language), a Gutenberg Bible, the world's biggest book (the 5ft tall Klencke Atlas), the journals of Captain Cook, and a crumpled piece of paper on which Paul McCartney scrawled the first lyrics to *Help*. But, most precious of all, you can experience something not easily found elsewhere in this chaotic city – silence. It's golden.

British Library, 96 Euston Rd; tel: 020 7412 7454; www.bl.uk; Mon–Fri 9.30am–6pm, to 8pm Tue, Sun 11am–5pm; map D5

Sup champagne in the marvel of 19th-century engineering that is St Pancras Station

Whether you have train tickets in your pocket or not, stopping at the Champagne Bar in St Pancras Station is a truly romantic experience. The bar runs alongside the international platform, and the mere idea that you could hop on one of those handsome trains and be in Paris in a few hours is a thrill in itself, while the station with its enormous vaulted roof is a wonder of the Victorian age to admire over a glass of bubbly. There is a long list of Champagne and some good breakfast and all-day snacking dishes. Don't forget to dress warmly if visiting in winter. There are powerful heaters beneath the seating, but it can still get chilly in this great glass railway shed.

St Pancras also houses a shopping arcade which has a well-stocked branch of **Hamleys** that those needing to buy gifts for children should note. And for adult gifts, there is **Oliver Bonas** with its quirky selection of clothes, accessories and homewares. Foodies whose time is too limited to get to Borough Market *(p.127)* should visit **Sourced**, Borough in miniature, but with particular emphasis on the Anglo-French links, with *boulangerie* from France and baked goods from Flour Power; cheeses from Neal's Yard and Mons *fromagerie*; hams and sausages from the Ginger Pig butchers and *charcuterie* from across France.

Champagne Bar, St Pancras Station, Pancras Rd; tel: 020 7870 9900; www. searcystpancras.co.uk; map D5

Get to know **Sir John Soane**, an obsessive art collector, and his **myriad curious artefacts**

Going to Sir John Soane's Museum is a pretty eccentric, very British experience. It is a narrow space so crammed with precious things that unless you go early you might be asked to wait in a queue outside until enough people have exited to allow you entrance. Before you go in, a smartly dressed usher will politely and firmly tell you to take off all hanging bags and put them in a carrier bag to decrease the risk of you accidentally knocking anything over. And if you ask a member of staff where the Canaletto paintings are, they might inform you to locate the statue of Apollo, lower your gaze, and, 'the landscapes are to the left of his bottom'.

Sir John Soane was an architect, most notably of the Bank of

England, but he is best known for his hobby – collecting art and antiquities. Soane collected so many during his lifetime (1753–1837) that his house was known as the 'academy of Architecture'. One of his proudest acquisitions was an alabaster sarcophagus found in Egypt's Valley of the Kings. The British Museum decided not to buy it, allowing Soane to snatch it up, a purchase that so elated him he threw a party that lasted three days. That's the kind of guy he was, and to visit this jewel-box of a house-museum is to take a trip into one man's obsessions. On the first Tuesday of every month, the museum is open until 9pm and lit by candles, making it an even more spookily atmospheric place to admire a gargoyle, a mummified cat or an ancient treasure.

Nearby is one of London's nicest independent coffee bars, **Fleet River Bakery**, where all the food – heavenly cakes, good bread, yummy soup, salads and quiches – is freshly baked or made from scratch on the premises every day.

Sir John Soane's Museum, 13 Lincoln's Inn Fields; tel: 020 7405 2107; www.soane. org; Tue–Sat 10am–5pm; free; map F2
Fleet River Bakery, 71 Lincoln's Inn Fields; map F2

Take a **tour of the greatest civilisations** of the world at the **British Museum**

The Great Court at the British Museum is the largest enclosed courtyard in Europe, and, with its magnificent glass roof, is a fittingly grand entrance to one of the greatest displays of antiquities in the world. There are eight million objects here that between them document the rise and fall of all the greatest civilisations. 'Only' about 80,000 of them are on display, but to do it all justice and have even the quickest squint at every one would take years. Here follows a suggested tour covering all areas which can be done in half a day:

Start in **Ancient Civilisations** on the ground floor, reached via the Great Court. Room 4 has the Egyptian sculptures including a magnificent bust of Rameses II, and the Rosetta Stone, which was discovered by Napoleon's army in the Nile Delta and provided the key to deciphering Egyptian hieroglyphs.

Next up are the Greeks in Gallery 18 and the Elgin Marbles – an exquisitely detailed frieze from the colonnade of the Parthenon.

Go up the West Stairs and into the **Ancient Near East** rooms where you can see beautiful Turkish and North African mosaics on your way through to the **Egyptian Galleries** (62 and 63) where the mummies lie resplendent and you can learn all about how it was done thanks to an at-a-glance guide on the wall by the door. Walking swiftly on, you will reach gallery 56 and find the magnificent *Babylonian Queen of the Night*, a generously curved woman on a clay plaque. Walk back through galleries 63 and 66 to reach the North Stairs which are dominated by the giant Chinese figure of the Amitabha Buddha.

In Room 40 tacticians and gameplayers should stop to admire the 11th-century Lewis Chessmen. Descend to the **Hotung Gallery** (33) to see a gracefully expressive gilt-and-bronze statue of the Buddhist goddess Tara from Sri Lanka. Exit the Hotung gallery and walk downstairs into the **Wellcome Trust Gallery** (24) to see the sacred if rather grumpy aspect of the Easter Island Statue. And don't miss the Mexican sculpture of Tlazolteotl

in Room 27 before returning to the Great Court and perhaps grabbing a coffee and sandwich over which to recover and reflect on all that you have seen.

You shouldn't leave, however, without a quick look round the **Enlightenment Gallery**. If you only have time for one room this would be a wise one to pick. It celebrates the great age of discovery when British naturalists, historians and scholars scoured the world for objects to help them to better understand life as it is, and was, lived. There is a replica of the Rosetta Stone that you are allowed to touch, and a hands-on table where you can have a feel of fossils, coins, arrowheads, tiles or pots. Don't forget to put them back.

British Museum, Great Russell St; tel: 020 7328 8181; www.britishmuseum. org; daily 10am–5.30pm; free; map D3

Take a walk in the **hidden tranquillity** of the **Inns of Court**

If you were accidentally beamed into the Inns of Court and told to guess where you were, you'd think you had landed in the quads of an ancient university. But this hidden enclave is where London barristers train and practise. There are four Inns – **Lincoln's Inn**, **Gray's Inn**, **Inner Temple** and **Middle Temple** – each with quiet gardens, medieval chapels and Tudor libraries and halls. And, despite some rather stern signs (one forbids the entrance of 'rude children'), you are welcome to pace the paths and picnic on the grass on weekdays (each Inn has slightly different entrance times,

so check websites). The halls are off bounds, unless you book a tour (London Walks; tel: 020 7624 3978) but the chapels are open to the public.

All the Inns of Court are steeped in history. The Jacobean poet, John Donne, was pastor of the Gothic Chapel at Lincoln's Inn, and his famous lines 'Never send to know for whom the bell tolls; it tolls for thee' were inspired by the bells that were rung to alert barristers of the death of one of their own. In 1601 Shakespeare oversaw the royal premiere of *Twelfth Night* at Middle Temple Hall where Queen Elizabeth I was a frequent guest. Dickens's first job was as a clerk in Gray's Inn, and he used the Tudor Hall in Lincoln's Inn as the setting for *Bleak House*. But whether you are interested in olden times or just want to rest a while in a peaceful garden – the Inns of Court are one of the city's most rewarding hidden treasures.

Inner Temple; tel: 020 7797 8250; www. innertemple.org.uk; map G1
Middle Temple; tel: 020 7427 4800; www.middletemple.org.uk; map G1
Lincoln's Inn; tel: 020 7405 1391; www. lincolnsinn.org.uk; map G2
Gray's Inn; tel: 020 7458 7800; www. graysinn.info; map G2

Savour the delights of a quirkily charming thoroughfare, **Lamb's Conduit Street**

Lamb's Conduit Street (LCS) is an enclave of independent shops. It does have a Starbucks on the corner to arouse the anti-globalisation warrior in you, but the rest of the street is pure London originals. And if variety is the spice of life, this street has a little bit of everything you fancy.

You could completely outfit yourself in LCS. **Oliver Spencer** (62) is mostly menswear of a cool, relaxed, military inspired kind, while **Folk** (49) sells affordable 'unrestrictive' modern leisure wear. **Pokit** (53) has womenswear, but is best loved for their accessories and range of British leather shoes. And there are two bespoke tailors, **Connock & Lockie** (33) and **Sims & MacDonald** (46), for suits made to suit you, sir.

For trinkets, nip round the corner to 13 Rugby Street to find the sky-blue **French's Dairy**. It was London's oldest dairy but is now a showroom for the best up-and-coming jewellery designers from around the world. You can feed yourself at **Kennards** (57), a grocer's overflowing with fabulous local, organic food – fish direct from Billingsgate, and organic vegetables from a farm in Surrey. Or feed your mind at **Persephone Books**, a publishing house with a mission to reprint neglected women writers such as Monica Dickens and Noel Streatfeild in beautifully designed editions. **Symphonic** (47) is a vinyl-only record store. **Matchless Prints** (36) has photography prints and books galore.

But for many, **The Lamb** (*pictured*) is the main attraction on LCS, a lovely old pub of the kind that are disappearing too fast and becoming relics of the past. **Cigala** (54) is a Spanish restaurant with great tapas. **Tutti's** (68) is a homely bustling café, and **Goodfellas** (50) is an NYC-style deli, only open for breakfast and lunch, that has a lovely shady back garden.

Tap into London's **literary treasure** at the **Charles Dickens Museum**

Barnaby Rudge, and father three children. This was a prodigious output by any standards, and you can detect some of the great man's intense energy as you admire the little desk beneath the window overlooking the back garden where he sat and wrote every day. The Charles Dickens Museum is one of the very few London attractions open on Christmas Day when they hold a candle-lit reading of *A Christmas Carol* to raise money for charity; an event of which Dickens would have heartily approved.

Dickens was an energetic and restless soul. He had several jobs before becoming the novelist and showman he is best known as. He followed many interests – philanthropic, theatrical and academic – to which he devoted much time and on which he wrote copious essays. He had ten children, one wife and several intense friendships with women about which there was much speculation. He moved his family into 48 Doughty Street in 1837. And though he only lived in it for two years, he managed in that time to complete *The Pickwick Papers*, write the whole of *Oliver Twist* and *Nicholas Nickleby*, commence

Fans of the most popular personality of the Victorian age in need of a pick-me-up should make a beeline for **Bea's of Bloomsbury**, a pretty little tearoom where they can enjoy good old-fashioned tea and cake with a very modern attitude towards the environment. All the ingredients are either locally sourced or brought in by sea freight, all waste is composted, and the energy is green. The brownies are to die for, but the salads are good too.

Charles Dickens Museum, 48 Doughty Street; tel: 020 7405 2127; www.dickens museum.com; daily 10am–5pm; map F4
Bea's of Bloomsbury, 44 Theobald's Road; tel: 020 7242 8330; map F3

Gain a little more understanding of the definition of London life at **Dr Johnson's House**

There are not many museums that have a definition of the month, but Dr Johnson's House does (at the time of going to press it was: 'strewment, any thing scattered in decoration'). But this is not surprising, as it was in the garret of this lovely early 18th-century town house that Dr Johnson laboured for nine years to produce the world's first comprehensive dictionary of the English language. Reproductions of the first edition with its 42,773 definitions lie open on the table in the study so you can choose your own favourite words. One phrase not in there is Tourette Syndrome, although Johnson with his frequent tics and involuntary gestures has been posthumously diagnosed with the condition. This is thought to be the reason he was unable to follow his chosen profession of teacher and was forced to become a writer, a job in which he could remain largely out of view, and unteased by children.

Johnson is perhaps most famous for having said: 'When a man is tired of London, he is tired of life.' And there is quite a lot of life in this house. Sadly Dr Johnson's beloved wife Elizabeth, or Tetty, died in 1752. Overcome with grief, his response was to fill his home with people. He took in random relatives and lodgers and surrounded himself with company. There are well-written and interesting explanatory cards in each room describing who lived there and the parties and activities that took place. It is a fascinating insight into a lost world. And if you want to take it outdoors, there is a walk around all Dr Johnson's favourite places – pubs and printing houses mostly – at 3pm on the first Wednesday of every month.

Dr Johnson's House, 17 Gough Square; tel: 020 7353 3745; www.drjohnsons house.org; Mon–Sat 11am–5.30pm, Oct–Apr until 5pm; map G2

Tuck into the authentic British **fish and chips** experience at the **Fryers' Delight**

Time was, fish and chips were the only fast food in Britain. Before kebab shops, curry houses, pizza places or McDonald's, if you wanted something cheap and speedy it was going to have to be deep-fried fish and potatoes. And there are times when, even despite all the wonders of global cooking that are currently available to you, fish and chips are still the only thing that will do.

If you are curious as to what made this, now somewhat overlooked, national dish once reign supreme then look no further than The Fryers' Delight. This long-time cabbies' favourite has been run by the same Italian family since 1968. And little has changed. They use the same suppliers they did 40-odd years ago, the chips are still good and chunky, the fish still comes in freshly whipped-up beer batter and everything is fried to order in beef dripping. Add a portion of mushy peas and a steaming cup of tea and you have the full works. The booth seating and formica tables are a very retro, cheerful setting for what must rank among the freshest, tastiest plates of fish and chips in the capital.

Fryers' Delight, 19 Theobald's Road; tel: 020 7405 4114; closed Aug; map F3

SOME OTHER GREAT PLACES FOR FISH AND CHIPS IN LONDON
Fish Bone, 82 Cleveland Street; tel: 020 7580 2672; map p.84 B3
Rock & Sole Plaice, 47 Endell Street; tel: 020 7836 3785; map p.47 F5
North Sea Fish Restaurant, 7–8 Leigh Street; tel: 020 7387 5892; map p.84 D4
Golden Hind, 73 Marylebone Lane; tel: 020 7486 3644; map p.24 B6
Seafresh Fish Restaurant, 80–81 Wilton Road; tel: 020 7828 0747; map p.66 D1
Sea Shell, 49–51 Lisson Grove; tel: 020 7224 9000; map p.25 A8
Fishcotheque, 79a Waterloo Road; tel: 020 7928 1484; map p.122 B3
fish! Kitchen, Bedale St, Borough Market; tel: 020 8468 1492; map p.123 E4

Discover **one-of-a-kind shops** in historic buildings

This is just a guess, but it's possible you might need an umbrella while in London. If you forgot to pack one or fancy buying a special new one, proceed directly to **James Smith & Sons** (53 New Oxford St; map E2), which has been in business since 1830. The shop is packed to the gunwales with umbrellas of all shapes, sizes and colours. Some of them are still made on the premises, and you can watch as one of the staff stitches the handmade items together. They cost from around £20, so if you do buy one, try not to leave it on the tube the next day.

You are unlikely to actually need a toy, but they are always nice to look at. Especially at **Pollock's Toy Museum and Toy Shop** (1 Scala St; map C3), which takes up two four-storey 18th-century houses and is most famous for its collection of Victorian model theatres. Children love looking at the weird and wonderful playthings of the past, and there's a shop next door selling modern replicas of many of them.

A little further afield is **The Old Curiosity Shop** (3–14 Portsmouth St; map F2). On the outside it is what it says – the shop built in 1567 immortalised by Dickens. On the inside, all is not quite what you'd expect. It has the quirky sloping roof and wonky, creaking floors of yore, but there are no London knick-knacks, no souvenirs, no Dickens memorabilia. Since 1992, this has been the showcase of the beautiful handmade shoes of Japanese designer Daita Kimura who has designed shoes for Vivienne Westwood and Yohji Yamamoto.

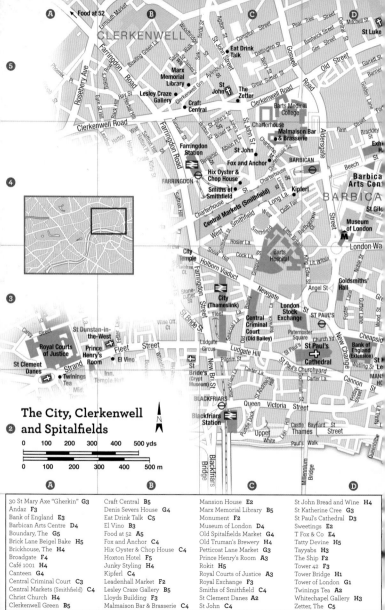

The City, Clerkenwell and Spitalfields

0 100 200 300 400 500 yds

0 100 200 300 400 500 m

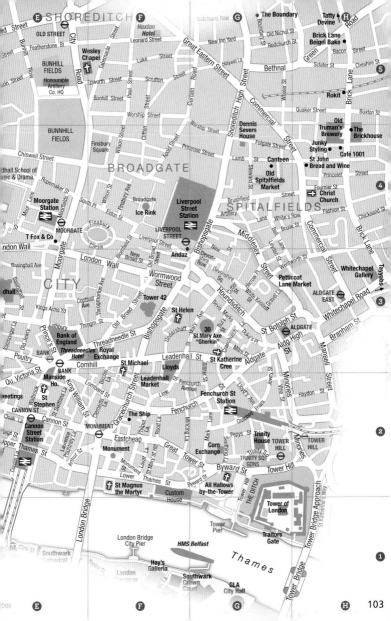

Find religion, revolution and jewels in
Clerkenwell Green

Clerkenwell Green is a discreet, almost hidden square that incongruously combines ancient knights, foreign revolutionaries and trendy craftspeople. It has been continuously inhabited for centuries. On the northern edge of the green you can still see remnants of the medieval well from which Clerkenwell gets its name, and relics of the 11th-century St John's church and hospital, just off it on St John's Lane. The 16th-century **Priory of the Knights of St John of Jerusalem** that was built to replace that church still stands, and there is a small museum devoted to the history of the Order of St John and the Knights Templars who would gather on Clerkenwell Green before setting off on their crusades. The oldest building currently standing on Clerkenwell Green was built in 1737 as a charity school and now houses the **Marx Memorial Library**. Marx's friend Lenin produced a magazine, *Iskra*, here, and the little room where he laboured has been saved for posterity and is open to the public, as is the library.

In the 18th century Clerkenwell Green was the centre of the English watchmaking industry, and there are still precision instrument makers and jewellers in the area. **Craft Central** is a not-for-profit association dedicated to preserving the nature of Clerkenwell and providing cheap workspaces for jewellers and watchmakers. They have regular open days and 'Made in Clerkenwell' exhibitions. Check their website for details. **The Lesley Craze Gallery** shows and sells work by more than 100 designers and is recognised as one of the foremost contemporary jewellery galleries in Europe. (Wendy Ramshaw's *Blue Knight*, left, was a piece specially commissioned for the gallery's 25th anniversary in 2009.)

Marx Memorial Library, 37a Clerkenwell Green; tel: 020 7251 4706; www.marx-memorial-library. org; Mon–Thur 1–6pm; free
Craft Central, 21 Clerkenwell Green; www.craftcentral.org.uk
The Lesley Craze Gallery, 33–35a Clerkenwell Green.
All map B5

Learn new culinary skills at a **Clerkenwell cookery school**, run in a stylish Georgian house

Over the past two decades, London has become a food destination as worthy of your inquiring palate as Paris or Rome. You can find food from all over the world, as well as exciting and inventive modern British food. So instead of just going out to eat, why not roll up your sleeves and play chef yourself?

Food at 52 is a cookery school run in the beautiful home of John Benbow (a former set designer and furniture maker). The courses you can choose from are Italian, Thai, Moroccan, Spanish, Lebanese, Fish and seafood, and best for those who just need to get some kitchen confidence, there is one called Stress-free Dinner Parties in which you learn to make two starters, two main courses and two desserts. John encourages each class to be a happy gang making the pasta or the noodles or the squid rings together, rather than standing in front of everyone demonstrating each task. Courses start at 10am with coffee and biscotti and end at around 3pm after a delicious lunch that you and your classmates have prepared yourselves.

Another nearby cookery school, **Eat Drink Talk**, runs an evening class on that uniquely British cooking genre, Gastro-pub cuisine.

Food at 52, 52 Great Percy St; tel: 07814 027 067; info@foodat52.co.uk; map A5
Eat Drink Talk, Unit 102, 190 St John St; tel: 020 7689 6693; www.eatdrinktalk.myshopify.com; map C5

Restaurant-hop your way around London's last-surviving meat market in **Smithfield**

In *Oliver Twist*, Dickens described Smithfield Market as being 'ankle deep in filth and mire', but don't let this put you off. Smithfield is still a working market, one of London's oldest, where meat has been bought and sold for over 800 years. However, it has managed to put aside its unseemly reputation for blood and filth and become a restaurant-rich playground for the young and hungry.

St John (26 St John St; tel: 020 7251 0848/4998) is perhaps the most famous of Smithfield restaurants. Opened in 1994 in a former smokehouse, it is presided over by Fergus Henderson, whose 'nose-to-tail eating' has inspired chefs the world over. Diners lured by the lavish praise heaped on St John (awarded a Michelin star in 2009) may be surprised at the extreme modesty of the white-walled surrounds as well as the plainness of the food – the focus is on seasonal British ingredients, and they come simply cooked and presented. The roast bone marrow with parsley is the most famous dish and has quite a following, as does the dessert plate of Eccles cake with Lancashire cheese, but you can also find excellent fish and unusual vegetables. **St John Bread and Wine** (94–96 Commercial St; tel: 020 7251 0848) is a more relaxed, informal outpost where you can pick up a loaf and a bottle on your way to a picnic or stop in for a bacon sandwich or meal.

Smith's of Smithfield (67–77 Charterhouse St; tel: 020 7251 7950) is on four storeys, each with a different offering – there's a buzzing bar with decent pub food on the ground floor where you cannot book but have to dive on a table as soon as it is vacated; a brasserie on the second floor; a lounge on the third; and a restaurant with a wraparound terrace on the fourth where the atmosphere is serene and the star is British beef.

British produce is also the focus at **Hix Oyster & Chop House** (35–37 Greenhill's Rents; tel: 020 7017 1930). Overseen by Mark Hix, former chef of the Ivy (*p.60*), and author of the highly influential recipe book, *British Regional Food,* it combines no-nonsense dining with occasional flourishes of old-fashioned white-tableclothed and silver-plated British class.

For more down-home food try **The Fox and Anchor** (115 Charter-house St; tel: 020 7250 1300), a great British pub with great British pub food. The hearty pies are immensely popular and the daily roast comes on a silver tray.

And now for something completely different – **Kipferl** (70 Long Lane, Farringdon; tel: 020 7796 2229) is a hip Austrian café that taps into that nation's historic talent for excellent coffee and cake, as well as sausages – and local office workers form long queues for the goulash soup. Or , if you have children to please, go all-American and take them to **Tinseltown** (44 St John St; tel: 020 7869 2424).

Smithfield; map C4

Shop by day and bar-hop by night in
Brick Lane

It's no wonder that Monica Ali chose this run-down cobbled East London street as lead character for her award-winning novel, *Brick Lane*. It tells quite a story, with its mix of elegant houses built by the Huguenots, synagogues, and sari shops; a tale of successive waves of immigrants and changing fortunes. For most of the last century the only reasons to come here were the large chaotic Sunday market or a cheap curry. But since the 1990s, galleries, boutiques, cafés, clubs and clever spaces that seem to cover all bases have been springing up. You're never short of things to do – whether you've come to hunt for vintage treasure *(see box)* or make a night of it.

If you're seeking a snack either side of midnight, try the 24-hour

Brick Lane Beigel Bake (159) for warm, fresh bagels that make you vow never to buy them from a supermarket ever again. **Café 1001** (91) dishes up breakfast, coffees and beats to E1's starving artists. **The Brickhouse** (152c) supper club has dinner with burlesque, cabaret and magic performances, and dancing until 2am.

The southern end of Brick Lane is still very much 'Banglatown', full of curry houses and men trying to beguile you into one. Those in the know walk straight past, heading for the nigh legendary **Tayyabs** (83 Fieldgate St; tel: 020 7247 9543) with its cheap but wonderful smoky grilled meats, selection of dhals and oven-baked breads.

Brick Lane; map H3–H5

VINTAGE BOUTIQUES
Dedicated followers of fashion should check out the following: **Tatty Devine** (236 Brick Lane) for gorgeous cheeky costume jewels; **This Shop Rocks** (131 Brick Lane) for handmade one-offs and vintage classics; **Junky Styling** (The Old Truman Brewery, 91 Brick Lane) for customised vintage; **The Laden Showroom** (103 Brick Lane) for young designers at the cutting edge; **Rokit** (101 & 107 Brick Lane), possibly London's biggest collection of vintage.

Work out where the next Picasso or Hirst is coming from at the **Whitechapel Gallery**

The Whitechapel Gallery was founded by young clergyman, Samuel Barnet, in 1901, who saw it as a way of bringing light to the people of East London and lifting them out of their grinding poverty. Although originally intended as a local gallery, the Whitechapel has made its name with an unerring eye for the best of the avant-garde, and for exhibiting emerging artists from around the world. It hosted Picasso's scathing anti-war painting *Guernica* on its world tour in 1939. In 1956, it was the first place to show Pop Art in London. It then went on, over the years, to introduce Jackson Pollock, Mark Rothko, Robert Rauschenberg and Frieda Kahlo to Britain. The Whitechapel also has a strong record of supporting fledgling British talent: Bridget Riley, David Hockney, Gilbert and George, and Antony Gormley all had important solo shows here that helped to establish their reputations.

In 2009, the Whitechapel had a £13 million refit, giving it an even more inviting space. They really wanted to bring back their most famous former exhibit for the re-opening, but *Guernica* has long been deemed too frail to travel from its home in Madrid's Reina Sofia. However, they did unveil a tapestry copy by Polish artist Goshka Macuga. In addition to the first-floor café there is now also a bright and attractive restaurant on the ground floor.

Whitechapel Gallery, 77–82
Whitechapel High St; tel: 020 7552 7888;
www.whitechapelgallery.org; Tue–Sun
11am–6pm, Wed until 9pm; free; map H3

Climb up to the **Whispering Gallery** and marvel at the magnificence of **St Paul's Cathedral**

So much of London was lost in the Great Fire of 1666, a shocking few days of devastation. But perhaps one thing modern Londoners should be glad for the loss of is the St Paul's Cathedral then on this site, because it allowed Sir Christopher Wren to come up with its replacement. He originally devised a scheme considered so radical and overreaching that it had to be toned down, and is said to have wept when forced to reduce the grandeur of his plan. Nevertheless, of the 50 churches he built after the Great Fire, St Paul's remains his masterpiece.

The best way to start a visit is to go directly to the centre, stand under the dome, and look around. This affords the best view before you go off exploring every nave and cranny. If you plan to climb the dome, do it now while you still have inclination and energy. Three hundred steps up a winding staircase later, you emerge into the whispering gallery, so called because the faintest whisper in one spot can be heard across the huge circle at the spot exactly opposite. Hold on to the railings and look down on the cathedral floor 30 metres below. It's an awesome sight. A further 231 steps up is the golden gallery from which you can see the whole of London laid out like a buffet.

St Paul's Cathedral, Ludgate Hill; tel: 020 7236 4128; www.stpauls.co.uk; Mon–Sat 8.30am–4.30pm; map D3

Drink champagne atop the city at **Vertigo 42**

You can't get much more exclusive than Vertigo 42. Visitors go through airport-style security checks before being allowed up to this sky-high champagne bar. And there are only 70 seats so you have to book ahead. Ask for the seats nearest the elevator to ensure the best view. Not that any view is bad: whichever side you sit on will cause a gasp, as might the price list, with bottles of champagne starting at £50, and glasses of wine around £8. But there are not many places you can drink in a view this fine. And drinks are the thing here – bar food is a small list of items such as smoked salmon, ham and pickle, or mushrooms on toasted brioche.

For a complete contrast, head over to the **Brasserie de Malmaison** in Smithfield for dinner. It's in a basement and exudes plush subterranean glamour with its velvet booths and delicious 'home-grown' menu.

Vertigo 42, International Financial Centre, Tower 42, 25 Old Broad St; tel: 020 7877 7842; www.vertigo42.co.uk; Mon–Fri noon–4pm, Mon–Sat 5–11pm, last reservation 9.45pm; map F3 Brasserie de Malmaison, 18–21 Charterhouse Square; tel: 020 7012 3700; map C4

THE FINEST MODERN BUILDINGS IN THE CITY

As you cast your eyes mistily around the historic sights at Vertigo 42, spare a glance for the City's world-class modern architecture too.
The Gherkin: Officially called 30 St Mary Axe, this 80-metre building is London's best-loved skyscraper.
Lloyd's Building: By Richard Rogers, the architect of Paris's Centre Pompidou, this glass-and-steel structure wears its services gracefully on the outside.
One Canada Square: You can see the distinctive Canary Wharf tower, with the pyramid hat, from most places in London. It is the UK's tallest building (or it was at the time of going to press, though several new buildings, including the Shard at London Bridge, are set to overtake it).

Take refreshment in the **11th-century crypt** of Sir Christopher Wren's **St Mary-Le-Bow**

This beautiful little church has the Great Bells of Bow which according to the popular nursery rhyme *Oranges and Lemons* say 'I do not know' to the bells of Stepney's question 'Pray when will that be?' They are also the bells that, if you are born within earshot of them, define you as a cockney or a true Londoner. The Bow Bells crashed to the ground when the church was bombed during the Blitz, but have since been restored on high without any damage to their lovely sound. And listeners to the BBC World Service may know that sound as it's their chime that punctuates the hours. But there is more to St Mary-Le-Bow than bells, for it's a beautiful place to sit and reflect. Sir Christopher Wren based his design on Rome's Basilica of Maxentius, and apart from the elaborate bell tower it has a restrained elegance unusual in his churches. Another very good reason to visit is **The Café Below**, in the crypt, which has delicious daily soups, salads, stews and specials, all of it made in the busy open-plan kitchen from organic local sources.

And if that puts pep in your step, you might want to consider the 311 steps at the nearby **Monument**. Built to commemorate the loss of buildings and life caused by the Great Fire, a climb up this beautiful, simple Doric pillar richly rewards you with a breathtaking view illustrating just how the city has regenerated itself since the days of London's Burning. Oh, and you get a certificate for your troubles.

St Mary-Le-Bow, The Place Below, Cheapside; tel: 020 7329 0789; www. cafebelow.co.uk; 7.30am–9pm; map D3 The Monument, Fish Street Hill; www. themonument.info; daily 9.30am–5.30pm; map F2

Catch a **concert**, film, exhibition or play at the **Barbican Centre**

The running joke about the Barbican Centre has been that as big as it is (and it is the largest arts centre in Europe) you could never find it. The vast concrete complex was built on a gaping site that had been bombed in World War II. Despite numerous design problems – wind moans through the walkways, it is easy to get lost, the concrete was the wrong type and requires constant maintenance – it is still Britain's finest example of Brutalist concrete architecture, unrivalled for its scale. At the heart of a residential complex comprising 2,000 flats, the Barbican arts centre is a cultural cornucopia, including an art gallery, theatre, cinema, library and the London Symphony Orchestra.

The Waterside Café has a terrace next to the Barbican Lake, and is great place to catch a little quiet time, watching the fountains and waterfall, moorhen and herons, and all the cute little ducks wandering around.

The Barbican Centre, Silk Street; tel: 020 7638 4141; www.barbican.org.uk; map D4

Be dazzled by the historical bling at the
Tower of London

When William the Conqueror began building his white stone tower in the middle of his London fortress in the 1070s, he wanted it not only to dominate the London skyline, but also the hearts and minds of his subjects. Even William, with his unending ambition and ruthless methods, would be amazed at how successful he has been in this. Nearly a thousand years later the White Tower still stands proud and is one of London's World Heritage Sites. With its mere three storeys, William's 'massive tower' has been seriously overshadowed by towers of a completely different kind all around it, but it continues to speak eloquently of Britain's history to the two million people a year who walk its halls.

The Armoury Room showing the knights and horses in their shining suits of armour is really awe-inspiring, as is St John's Chapel – one of the best-preserved Anglo-Norman churches in Britain. However, most people come to the Tower of London to gawp at **The Crown Jewels** – all the tiaras, crowns, orbs and sceptres owned and sported by British royalty for the past 700 years are twinkling away on display here, and it is wise to pick an early arrival to this part of your tour, because at peak times the crowds can slow you down somewhat. Another treat is the view over the ramparts to the River Thames from the East Wall walk. Watch out for the Royal Ravens; legend has it that, if they ever leave, the tower will crumble.

For refreshment, seek out the **Most Café** hidden in the base of Tower Bridge (p.124).

Tower of London, Tower Hill; tel: 020 3166 6000; www.hrp.org.uk/ TowerOfLondon; Tue–Sat 9am– 5.30pm, Sun–Mon 10am–5.30pm; charge; map G1

Dig deep into the city's **archaeological layers** at the **Museum of London**

London is not just a big city with a long history, it is an intensely complicated and multi-layered place – made up of peoples from all over the world living in villages joined together into a huge metropolis and affected in varying ways by centuries of history. Nowhere is this more apparent than in the new basement galleries of the Museum of London, which aim to tell the tumultuous, dramatic story of London and its people from 1665 to the present day. It is a story of constantly being knocked down and picking itself up again; of destruction and reinvention such as that brought about by the plague, or the Great Fire or the Blitz.

A 240-year-old printing press spills news stories across the gallery ceiling in a clever collision of new and old technologies. And all the while you are walking over glass cases holding the city's archaeology underfoot. There is all the glamour of the theatre (lots of lavish costumes) and commerce (an amazing Art Deco lift that once raised shoppers in Selfridges) but this is counterbalanced by a room filled with the voices of London's dispossessed so you can also take in the meaning of a life of poverty in the shadows

of one of the richest cities in the world. To take you really up to the minute, there is an innovative multimedia piece, LND24, screened on a 160ft elliptical LED screen that explores a 24-hour cycle of London life with 35 live feeds following the pulse of the city. There's also an interactive installation comprised of a constantly changing collage of hundreds of photographs submitted by Londoners.

Museum of London, London Wall; tel: 020 7001 9844; www.museumoflondon. org.uk; daily 10am–6pm, free; map D4

Bag anything from a piece of **contemporary art to chic vintage clothing** to a tasty pie at **Spitalfields**

The market at Spitalfields is on all week, but the best day to visit is Sunday when you get the widest variety of stalls. Largely regarded as a showcase for up-and-coming young artists from the nearby art and design college, Spitalfields Market has lots of vintage, retro and modern original clothes. It is also very strong on jewellery and has stalls selling every style of human adornment you can imagine. It does get very busy on a Sunday though, so if you are crowd-shy come in the week when they have specifically tailored selections of stalls (if it's Tuesday, it's arts and crafts, Thursday is antiques, Friday is fashion) and far fewer people. Whenever you come, Spitalfields is chock-full of good things to eat and snacking opportunities, but if you are after a meal, go to **Canteen** (2 Crispin Place). This mini-chain is devoted to high-quality British food served in fashionably retro-modern surroundings. The prices are above the average works canteen, but then so are the taste and the quality – way, way above.

Just across the road from the market is **Christ Church Spitalfields** by Nicholas Hawksmoor, Sir Christopher Wren's most talented pupil, second only to him as architect of the city's finest churches.

Spitalfields, 65 Brushfield Street; tel: 020 7377 1496; www.visitspitalfields. com; map G4

THE EAST END'S SUNDAY MARKETS

Brick Lane: hundreds of stallholders selling a glorious muddle of bric-a-brac and desirable objets. Map H3–H5

UpMarket: indoor market at the Old Truman Brewery with vintage galore, music and crafts. Map H4

Petticoat Lane: Middlesex Street, cheap clothes and accessories and Asian fabrics. Map G3

Columbia Road: flowers, plants and all gardeners' delights plus cool cafés and boutique shops. Map p.159 F4

Time travel to the 18th and 19th centuries in the remarkable **Dennis Severs House**

London is full of house museums – the Dickens, the Handel, the Sir John Soane – which do a marvellous job of re-creating a moment in time and telling a story. But none of them transports you back in time the way Dennis Severs House does. The minute you walk into this remarkable house, inhabited by wealthy Huguenot silk weavers from 1724 until 1919 (by which time the silk trade was dying and they were no longer wealthy), your senses are bombarded – cold, dark, unfamiliar smells and faintly spooky sounds – and you are immersed in a real physical sense of the past. Severs, who died in 1991, wanted people to walk around the house in silence so that they could fully absorb the atmosphere, and there are still signs hand-painted by him with his motto, 'You either see it or you don't', in each of the 11 rooms which take you through the five generations of one family, the fictional Jervises, and from the Enlightenment with its strong bright colour schemes on the ground floor to the outbreak of World War I in the attic rooms. A truly remarkable experience.

Dennis Severs House, 18 Folgate St; tel: 020 7247 4013; www.dennissevershouse. co.uk; map G4

Catch a **number 15** bus and get a bird's-eye view of London life from **St Paul's to Trafalgar Square**

Venice has its gondolas, Amsterdam its bikes, London its red buses. And one of the best buses for sightseeing is the number 15 Routemaster bus *(see box below)*. Pick it up in front of **St Paul's Cathedral** (map D3) on the opposite side of the street. Take the front seat on the top deck (if possible) for the best views. As the bus moves off, a glance to the left reveals the **Millennium Bridge** over the river to Tate Modern. Then look to the right and you will see the bell tower of **The Old Bailey**, the Central Criminal Court. Next, the bus turns into **Fleet Street**, centre of British printing since the 1500s. The newspapers and the presses are long gone, but nostalgic journalists still return to drink at **El Vino** (47 Fleet St; map B3). At the point where Fleet Street joins The Strand are the **Royal Courts of Justice**. Directly across the road is the original **Twinings Tea** (map B3), which has been selling infusions since 1706. The Strand, originally a bridle path running along the Thames, leads to **Trafalgar Square** (map p.65 F5). In front of Nelson's Column is a statue of Charles I which marks the centre of London, the point from which all distances to the capital are measured.

SIGHTSEEING BUS ROUTES
The number 15 is a **heritage route**. This means that the Routemaster runs it (or at least part of the service from Tower Hill to Trafalgar Square). This is the iconic red doubledecker, with the open door at the back and a conductor on board, which was put out of commission in 2005. The other heritage route is the **number 9** between Knightsbridge and Trafalgar Square. Another notable bus is the **RV1**. This is a single-decker 'bendy bus', but runs from Tower Bridge along the South Bank, across Waterloo Bridge and into Covent Garden. For maps and information, contact Transport for London; tel: 0843 222 1234; www.tfl.gov.uk.

A **glittering bar** and **glimmering shops** at the Royal Exchange

During the 17th century, stockbrokers were not allowed in the Royal Exchange due to their 'rude manners'. Nowadays it is open to all as, since 2001, it has been reinvented as a luxury shopping mall full of bijoux boutiques wrapped around the smart brasserie at its centre. Which is very apt as this grand, Grade I-listed building has always been a temple to London's wealth. In the centre of the soaring atrium is a gleaming bar and seafood counter, but the best tables are on the first-floor gallery overlooking the action. The posh shops at Royal Exchange are mostly devoted to jewels, fashion and fragrance with Tiffany, Cartier, Tateossian and Bulgari; Jo Malone, Gucci, Hermes, Paul Smith and Lulu Guinness – it's rather like a mini version of Bond Street without traffic or rain to contend with.

If you want to fit yourself out like one of those 'rude' stockbrokers, try **T Fox and Co** which has all a City gent's requirements from silk socks to handmade ties. And to nosh like one, try **Sweetings**, the lunch-only establishment that has been serving gulls' eggs, wild salmon, soused herring and grilled lobsters to City types since 1889.

The Royal Exchange (where Cornhill and Threadneedle St meet); www.the royalexchange.com; store: 10am–6pm, restaurants and bars: 8am–11pm; map F3
T Fox and Co, 118 London Wall; map E4
Sweetings, 39 Queen Victoria St; tel: 020 7248 3062; map E2

Bankside, South Bank and Waterloo

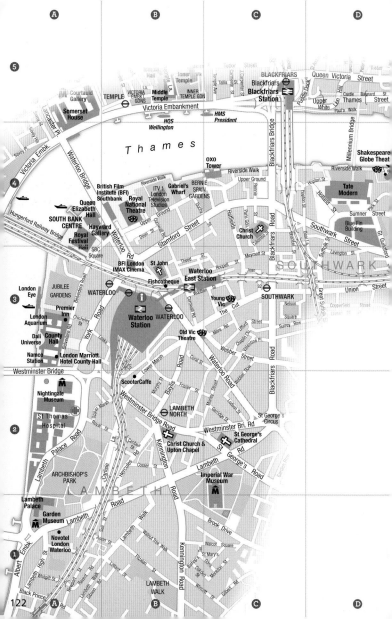

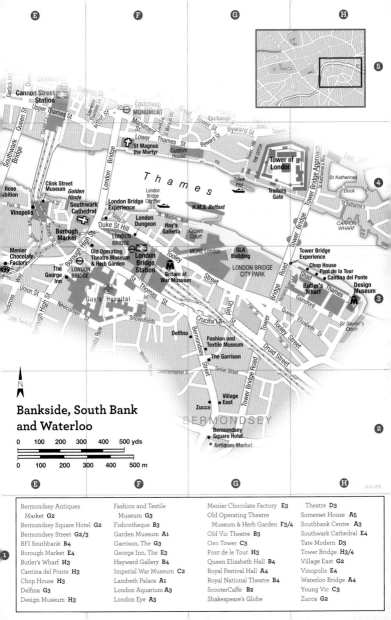

Bankside, South Bank and Waterloo

Absorb an **iconic view** from London's most famous river crossing, **Tower Bridge**

The silhouette of Tower Bridge is second only to Big Ben as the most recognisable symbol of London. When it was unveiled in 1894, Tower Bridge was at the cutting edge of modern technology. Even now, watching the bridge opening up is to understand why London was once the most technologically advanced city in the world.

It is a suspension bridge, but is also equipped with a massive bascule (seesaw) mechanism that swings into life and raises the two sides of the bridge in three minutes flat to allow oncoming shipping through. In 1997, a lifting famously separated President Clinton from his motorcade. Clinton had had lunch with then British Prime Minister, Tony Blair, at Pont de la Tour (*see opposite*), and arrived at the bridge just as it was lifting.

Although London's days as a thriving port are long gone, 40,000 people a day cross the bridge and it still gets to strut its stuff lifting around 1,000 times a year. To find out when the next lifting will be, call or check the website.

You can also tour the engine rooms to see how it works and walk the high walkways for some of the best views of the river.

It's not immediately visible from the bridge, but there's a bar hidden in its base. The **Most Café Bar** is a great place to nurse a drink and watch the world drift by.

Tower Bridge; tel: 020 7940 3984; www.towerbridge.org.uk; map H3/4
Most Café Bar, Shad Thames; tel: 020 7403 6030; www.mostcafebar.co.uk; map H3

A definitive collection of **modern classics** at the **Design Museum**

Before the Design Museum landed here in 1989, this stretch of the river just east of Tower Bridge was little visited and less loved. But since then it has been much gentrified, and Sir Terence Conran, whose idea the Design Museum was, has turned the adjacent Butler's Wharf into a stylish dining destination *(see box below)*. And the Design Museum, in its white 1940s Bauhaus-esque former banana warehouse, is still an important draw to the area with its dynamic roster of exhibitions. These change frequently and cover all aspects of modern design, from the shoes of Manolo Blahnik to children's comics to F1 cars. The permanent collection is situated in the museum's store, where you can buy desirable objects. There's also a snug spot for coffee on the ground floor as well as a more extensive (and, of course, more expensive) place, **The Blueprint Café**, on the top floor, with gorgeous views across the Thames.

The Design Museum, 28 Shad Thames; tel: 0207 403 6933; www.designmuseum. org; daily 10am–5.45pm; under-12s free; map H3

BUTLER'S WHARF

Sir Terence Conran, who opened British minds to continental design with the launch of his furniture emporium, Habitat, in the '60s, turned his hand to food in the '80s and totally transformed the London dining scene in the process. Nowhere more so than at Butler's Wharf where he has three restaurants in a row – **Le Pont de la Tour** for refined French seafood (tel: 020 7403 8403), the traditional British **Butler's Wharf Chop House** (tel: 020 7403 3403), and the Italian-leaning **Cantina del Ponte** (tel: 020 7403 5403) – all housed in a once derelict warehouse (36 Butler's Wharf) with outdoor terraces overlooking the Thames. If you are not in the mood for fine dining, you can have the same view and a similar terrace at **Brown's Bar & Brasserie** (tel: 020 7378 1700). *Map H3*

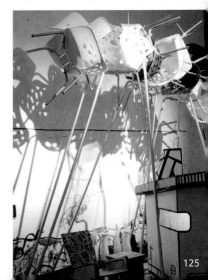

Sing the praises of **London's oldest Gothic building** at Southwark Cathedral

It may not look much from outside, particularly in a city graced with St Paul's Cathedral and Westminster Abbey, but Southwark Cathedral is far more beautiful on the inside. Properly known as Cathedral and Collegiate Church of St Saviour and St Mary Overie, Southwark, this is one of London's oldest places of worship. It is believed that there has been a church on this spot for over 1,000 years, and the remains of an altar to a Roman hunter god were unearthed here in the 1970s. A disastrous fire in 1212 badly damaged the earlier Norman church, traces of which can be seen in the nave. The cathedral was then rebuilt and is now London's oldest-standing Gothic building.

Southwark was the city's first theatre district, and the area's stage connections are reflected here with monuments to actors, poets and playwrights. A window in the south aisle commemorates William Shakespeare, depicting characters from all 36 of his plays. And students of early English literature will know that Geoffrey Chaucer's pilgrims set off from a nearby hostelry, The Tabard, in *The Canterbury Tales*. The Tabard no longer stands, but the neighbouring **George Inn** (*map E3*) is still there; and as London's last-remaining galleried coaching inn, it is well worth a visit.

The cathedral has a charming riverside **Courtyard Café** (10am–5pm), and there's an airy Refectory for rainy days. Sandwiches, salads and soups are good-value quick lunches, and there's also tea and cake.

One of the best things about Southwark Cathedral is the choir; do try to catch them in full song (check website for times).

Southwark Cathedral, Montague Close; tel: 020 7367 6700; www.cathedral. southwark.anglican.org; map E4

Discover the delights of a Chelsea bun and other **gourmet pleasures** at **Borough Market**

On Saturday mornings, it feels like all of London and a large chunk of the rest of the world's food-loving population have come to **Borough Market** to wander around and chomp on a sandwich, a sausage or some other gourmet delight. Borough is London's oldest covered fruit-and-veg market, and the go-to place for top chefs in search of premium ingredients and grazers looking for tasty treats. It's hard to think of anyone, however simple or exotic their tastes, going home disappointed. You can find everything here: artisan cheeses, cured hams, stuffed olives, truffle oil, foie gras, freshly pressed juices, oysters, fish and chips, kebabs, falafels, veggie burgers, chocolates, pastries and cakes, including the eccentric British Chelsea bun and Eccles cake. Standouts (with queues) are: the chorizo sandwich at Spanish specialist stall **Brindisa**, the fish finger sandwich at **fish!**, the grilled cheese or raclette at **Kappasein**, and the scallops and bacon at **Shellseekers**.

If you'd rather sit down, try breakfast at **Roast**, mid-morning coffee at **Monmouth Coffee House**, oysters and a pint of prawns at **Wright Brothers** or late lunch at **Brindisa** (the tapas bar).

But it's not all about the food. **Vinopolis** is the market's temple to the grape. This wine museum allows you to tour all the wine-growing regions of the world. There's enough information to make you drunk with facts, but there's plenty of delicious wine available on the tasting tables, making the pricey entrance fee somewhat more palatable.

There's also a vast selection of wines by the glass in the adjoining **Wine Wharf** and restaurant **Cantina Vinopolis**.

Borough Market, Southwark Street; Thur–Sat; www.boroughmarket.org.uk. Vinopolis, 1 Bank End; tel: 020 7940 8300; www.vinopolis.co.uk; Thur–Sat noon–10pm, Sun noon–6pm; map E4

Take a river walk from **Southwark Bridge to Westminster Bridge**

This riverside walk has an extraordinary collection of cultural institutions and interesting buildings lining one, traffic-free, thoroughfare. The walk begins beneath **Southwark Bridge** (map E4), decorated with tiled murals depicting the Frost Fairs that were held when the Thames froze over in 1814; the tradition has been revived and Frost Fairs are held on the South Bank every December. Just after you exit the bridge, look out for the steps once used by Thames watermen to await customers wanting to cross the river. Sandwiched between **the Globe** (p.131) and **Tate Modern** (p.130) is **Cardinals Wharf**, a tall sliver of a house built in 1710 bearing a plaque saying: 'Here lived Sir Christopher Wren during the building of St Paul's'. Don't

believe it – the house was built the year St Paul's was completed and it's thought the plaque was salvaged from a neighbouring, since-demolished, address. Next comes the **Millennium Bridge** (*pictured*). Even if you are not going to cross the footbridge, it is worth walking the ramp to the foot of it to gaze over – it gives the miraculous impression of holding St Paul's aloft on its span. Just after **Blackfriars Bridge** (named for the monks who lived on the north side during the Middle Ages) is **The Oxo Wharf**. Originally a power station, later a stock cube factory, it has been rebuilt to include 50 funky little design shops, restaurants and galleries. A little further on is the smaller, slightly hippier, **Gabriel's Wharf** with craft shops, bars and restaurants. Just after the halfway mark, **Waterloo Bridge** is a good place to stop and admire the view of the north bank. The last tree-lined stretch takes you past the **Southbank Centre** (p.134) to the **London Eye** (*opposite*) and County Hall which houses the **London Aquarium**, and finally to **Westminster Bridge**, painted green to reflect the green leather benches in the House of Commons (Lambeth Bridge down river is red for the House of Lords).

Take in a living, breathing **panorama** on the
London Eye

The London Eye has become a much-loved part of the landscape in a relatively short amount of time; almost as much a part of the city's identity as the Eiffel Tower is to Paris. The Eye also does the same trick as the Eiffel does for Paris. That is to let people climb above the city and look back down on it. And to think it was only meant to be there for a few years. The London Eye was originally put up as a way of celebrating the coming Millennium. But it was so popular — it attracts more than 3.5 million visitors a year — that it has been declared a permanent attraction. And no wonder. Once you have climbed into your space-agey steel and glass capsule,

the wheel's graceful 30-minute revolution takes half an hour, in which time you can see just how big London really is, and have the whole glorious 360-degree panorama of it at your feet.

The building directly behind it is **County Hall**, once the seat of London's local government, now home to restaurants, cafés and attractions including the not cheap but splendid **London Aquarium** with its spectacular tank of sharks.

The London Eye; tel: 0870 990 8883; www.londoneye.com. London Aquarium, County Hall; tel: 020 7967 8000; www. sealife.co.uk/london; Mon–Thur 10am–6pm, Fri–Sun 10am–7pm; map A3

Marvel at one of the world's most dynamic exhibition spaces, **the Turbine Hall at Tate Modern**

Tate Modern is an amazing story of redemption and reinvention. It resides in the former Bankside Power Station, a hulking monolith that closed in 1981 and was regarded as a monstrous blemish on the Thames skyline. So when it was mooted as a location for the Tate's world-class collection of modern art, the idea was received with scepticism. But, after an amazing makeover by Swiss architects Herzog & de Meuron, it is almost universally loved.

Its permanent display includes works from Matisse, Pollock and Picasso to Anish Kapoor and Tacita Dean – you name 'em, they've got 'em. They are arranged thematically, rather than chronologically or by artist, and you could happily spend a day exploring them all. However, most people come for the latest barnstorming exhibition. The biggest, most audacious, installations are in the vast Turbine Hall (*pictured*). The Material Gestures galleries on Level 3 feature an impressive offering of post-World War II painting and sculpture. Room 7 contains a breathtaking collection of Rothkos and Monets. The website has a 'my tour' planner, which allows you to print out a personalised map. Or join a free guided tour; they take 45 minutes and there's one for each gallery: Poetry and Dream at 11am, Material and Gestures at noon, States of Flux at 2pm, and Idea and Object at 3pm.

One of London's worst-kept secrets is that if you go to the **Tate Modern Restaurant** on Level 7 you can have coffee or lunch (and dinner on Fridays and Saturdays when the Tate stays open late) with one of the most stunning views of the Thames.

Tate Modern, Bankside; tel: 020 7887 8888; www.tate.org.uk/modern; Sun–Thur 10am–6pm, Fri–Sat 10am–10pm; free; map D4

Let the players entertain you at an **Elizabethan playhouse** and visit **Shakespeare's Globe**

There wouldn't be a Shakepeare's Globe if it wasn't for American movie director and actor Sam Wanamaker. Wanamaker began his acting career performing Shakespeare in a replica of the Globe at the Great Lakes' World Fair in Cleveland, Ohio. On a trip to London in 1949, he was amazed to discover that there was no commemoration of the Globe in the city and set about getting this faithful reconstruction built a stone's throw from the site of the original Elizabethan playhouse where most of Shakespeare's plays were first performed. Sadly, Wanamaker didn't live to see the Globe opened by the Queen in 1997, but more than 300,000 visitors a year come to watch a play, have a tour of the building or just to quaff an ale in the pub upstairs. Some very imaginative enactments of Shakespeare's canon are staged here, as well as plays by contemporary authors to enliven the roster. The season runs only during the warmer months, but the permanent exhibition (daily, May–Sept 9am–noon and 12.30–5pm, Oct–Apr 10am–5pm) devoted to the playwright's life and times is really rewarding.

Shakespeare's Globe Theatre, 21 New Globe Walk; tel: 020 7902 1400; www. shakespeares-globe.org; map D4

Climb a church tower and discover the fascinating if gory surrounds of the **Old Operating Theatre**

You need to negotiate an ancient, steep and rickety spiral staircase to get here, but this beautiful oak-beamed loft is one of London's most intriguing historical interiors. Hidden in the roof of a hospital chapel, this is the oldest surviving operating theatre in Europe, and don't worry, the patients didn't have to get up

here this way; the chapel roof once butted on to the women's ward of St Thomas's Hospital and they were wheeled in from there. However, in 1862, the 12th-century hospital buildings were knocked down to make way for London Bridge Station, and these rooms were boarded up and totally forgotten about until their rediscovery in 1956.

You will need to steel your nerves for some of the displays of bottled organs and body parts, and the cases of instruments used by the surgeons in the Victorian operating theatre are truly scary – many of them look much better suited to torture than to healing. None of it, however, is as terrifying as the thought that, until 1847, surgeons had no anaesthesia and depended on alcohol or opiates to dull the patient's senses. The less squeamish should check the website and make sure to attend one of the surgery demos staged by museum staff as these are both hilarious and amazingly enlightening on history, science and human fortitude.

Old Operating Theatre Museum and Herb Garret, 9a St Thomas's Street; tel: 020 7188 2679; www.thegarret.org.uk; daily 10.30am–5pm; map F3-4

Eat, shop and play with the in-crowd in London's hottest new destination, **Bermondsey Street**

Bermondsey has an edgy, undiscovered feel to it. The best way of exploring it is to start in the area's eponymous street where you can bag hip finds from small funky shops, and eat your way round the world in stylish pubs, restaurants and bars.

Start in Bermondsey Square where you can find the area's oldest attraction, the **Antiques Market**, on Friday mornings (5am–noon), alongside one of its newest, the sleek **Bermondsey Square Hotel**, which has an inviting brasserie/bar. Then, walking north towards London Bridge you will pass: **Pure and Applied** (169), a frame store with affordable prints, photographs and maps; **Zucca** (184), which has deceptively plain and exceptionally delicious Italian food in cool white surroundings; **Village East** (171–173), with a strong cocktail list and pretty good food too; and **Bermondsey 167** (167), a boutique strong on interesting Latin jewellery. At **Bermondsey Street Coffee** (162–167) you can lounge on sofas beneath chandeliers made of plastic coffee cups, and feast on goulash or salads. **United Nude Terra Plana** (127) has beautiful and environmentally kind shoes. Or pop in **Caphe House** (114) for Vietnamese coffee or a bowl of

fresh *pho*. **Holly and Lil** (103) has everything for the chic city dog. **The Garrison** (99) is a relaxed and beautifully restored gastropub – great for Sunday lunch. **The Cockfighter of Bermondsey** (96) is the place for sassy slogan T-shirts and saucy underpinnings. **Pussy Willow** (90) provides beautiful custom-made women's clothing. **The Fashion and Textile Museum** (83) cannot be missed in its striking orange and pink building, and **Delfina** (50) is the restaurant that kicked off the Street's renaissance. Originally the canteen for the artists who occupied the building, Delfina has been knocking out delicious Mediterranean food to the general public since 1994.

Bermondsey Street; map G2/3

133

Experience culture high and low in the galleries and halls inside and outside the **Southbank Centre**

The Southbank Centre is a 21-acre metropolitan arts centre with an extraordinary history. It all started in 1951 with the Festival of Britain. At that time, London was badly in need of redevelopment, and the Festival was described as a tonic for the nation. Warehouses and housing were cleared to make a new public space and the Festival buildings went up. It was a resounding success, but when Churchill got back into power in 1953, his government promptly razed all but the **Royal Festival Hall** for being 'too socialist'. However over the ensuing decades other cultural halls and exhibition spaces – the Queen Elizabeth Hall,

the Hayward Gallery, the Purcell Room and the Poetry Library – were added until the Royal Festival Hall became the beating heart at the centre of the Southbank. And whatever you think of the oft-criticised brutal modernist architecture, the Southbank is still a tonic for all. With three auditoriums hosting world-class orchestras, musical ensembles and dance performances, plus cutting-edge art exhibitions and outdoor performances, it is a constant hive of activity of the highest order.

On the river terrace there are branches of the classier fast-food chains such as Eat, Giraffe and Wagamama, and in the Festival

Hall there is **Skylon** for fine dining or classy drinking. And there's an outpost of Spitalfield's **Canteen** with its delicious British all-day dining menu. Not to be left out, the Hayward Gallery also has its very own arty bar and café, **Concrete**, with a rotating programme of the art installations du jour.

And if your brain hasn't exploded from overexposure to culture, just next door is the **Royal National Theatre**, with its three theatres and exciting roster of plays. If you haven't managed to get tickets to one of these you could take a behind-the-scenes tour of the three theatres. Alternatively, wander outside and catch the street theatre of the skate kids as they slam and pop up and down concrete steps and under the walkways.

Or walk along to the neighbouring **BFI Southbank** (home of the British Film Institute) which

has four cinema screens showing everything from Charlie Chaplin to Michael Haneke (plus a selection of the latest commercial releases, and filmed operas). BFI Southbank has a lovely relaxed café and bar, **Benugo**, with long low leather sofas that are often bedecked with romantic couples. If you have spare time between screenings browse the second-hand book stall on the terrace come rain or shine.

Southbank Centre, Belvedere Road; www.southbankcentre.co.uk.
Hayward Gallery, South Bank; tel: 020 7792 1081; www.hayward.org.uk; map A4
National Theatre, South Bank; tel: 020 7452 3000; www.nt-online.org; map B4
BFI Southbank, Belvedere Road; tel: 020 7928 3232; www.bfi.org.uk; map B4

See **stage and screen stars** tread the boards at **The Old Vic**

Many of the great names of British stage and screen – John Gielgud, Alec Guinness, Laurence Olivier, Judi Dench, Glenda Jackson, Anthony Hopkins – got their start or established their reputation at The Old Vic. So when, gasp, an American, the actor Kevin Spacey, was appointed artistic director in 2003 there were mixed reactions. Could a film actor, albeit such a fine one, from New Jersey really understand this revered theatre that for 200 years had been a driving force in British playmaking? His first year was shaky, but ever since then Spacey has been getting huge audiences. His overhaul has included more comfortable seats and a decent bar, and introducing the Bridge

Project, a scheme he hatched with Sam Mendes (formerly creative director of the Donmar Warehouse, *p.56*, and now a New York-based film director) and the Brooklyn Academy of Music. The idea was to enmesh the theatrical worlds of London, Broadway and Hollywood, and the result has been a series of productions of classic texts with stellar casts.

Around the corner is the marvellous **ScooterCaffe** (132 Lower Marsh, map B2) for coffee, snacks and drinks in the unusual surroundings of a scooter work-shop. And across the road is **The Young Vic**, a training ground for young directors, playwrights and actors, which has a much bigger and better café, **The Cut Bar**. Another dynamic small theatre in the area is **The Menier Chocolate Factory**, which specialises in quirky musicals, such as *La Cage aux Folles*, and new plays that frequently make it big and transfer to a West End theatre.

The Old Vic, The Cut; tel: 020 7902 7571; www.oldvictheatre.com; map B3
The Young Vic, The Cut; tel: 020 7922 2922; www.youngvic.org; map C3
Menier Chocolate Factory, 51 Southwark St; tel: 020 7378 1712; www. menierchocolatefactory.com; map E3

Tour the **Imperial War Museum** and discover that it is not just for gun-obsessed boys or war historians

Perhaps it is no accident that the grand structure in which the Imperial War Museum is housed was once Bethlem, a hospital for the care of the insane from which the word 'bedlam' comes. For the Imperial War Museum is a crazy kind of place that does a marvellous job of conveying the madness of war. If you go in the week it is likely to be full of parties of school children clambering up ladders to peer into bomber planes and crawling around reconstructed trenches.

Just watching the enthusiasm with which these armies of under-16s tackle the place shows how vibrant and alive a museum can be even if it is dedicated to grim and traumatic events. The Imperial War Museum has dedicated itself to living history rather than dusty cases of artefacts. So you don't just see photographs of bombed-out London streets; you can go and sit in a replica of a shelter and listen to the neighbours argue, a narrative punctuated by scarily realistic sounds of bombs falling. There are also changing exhibitions covering different aspects of war from the slightly glamorous espionage, to the more mundane – food and rationing.

Imperial War Museum, Lambeth Road; tel: 020 7416 5320; www.london.iwm.org. uk; daily 10am–6pm; free; map C2

137

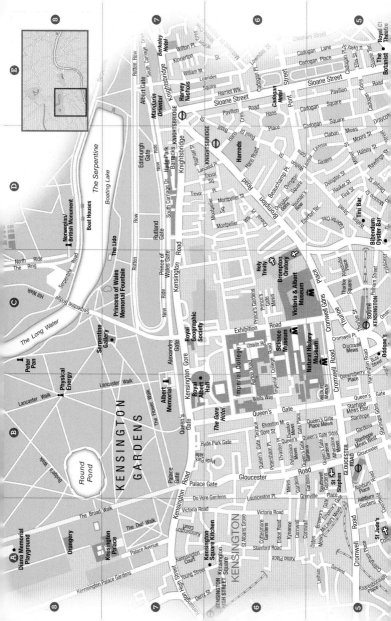

Kensington and Chelsea

Shop in luxury at the iconic emporium, **Harrods**, and its fashionista neighbour, **Harvey Nichols**

Harrods has 330 departments spread over 1 million square feet, so your visit requires as much precision planning as your trip to the British Museum. List the things you most want to see and work out a circuit (the website has a floor guide). Whether you are looking to buy a fossil, a dress, or a teddy bear sporting a Harrods logo sweater, you should also try to take in the beautiful tiled food halls, the Christmas Store (Aug 1–Dec 24) and the pet department.

And make use of Harrods' cafés and restaurants – 29 in total – to restore and re-energise as you make your way around this splendid emporium. These range from an Illy Espresso bar for quick recharges to a full pub, The Green Man, in the basement, and The Rotisserie on the ground floor which offers excellent people-watching as well as delicious flame-grilled meats and salads.

Fans of *Absolutely Fabulous* will know that 'Harvey Nicks' has a near fanatical following among London's fashionistas. Much smaller than its more famous neighbour, **Harvey Nichols** is the one that Knightsbridge 'Ladies who Lunch' could not do without. It has a great beauty hall, a divine food department and good

menswear and kids' departments, but its main attractions are women's fashion and accessories, both of which feature collections by hot young designers as well as elegant classics. Don't forget to admire the windows on your way in; they are cheeky and fun, and you can see Londoners on passing buses craning their necks to get a proper look at them.

Harrods, 87 Brompton Road; tel: 020 7730 1234; www.harrods.com; map D6
Harvey Nichols, 109-125 Knightsbridge; tel: 020 7235 5000; www.harveynichols. com; map E7. Both stores: Mon–Sat 10am–8pm, Sun 11.30am–6pm.

Study Sloane Rangers close up at **The Botanist**, **Bluebird** and **Bibendum Oyster Bar**

The Botanist is not, it has to be said, the most beautiful pub in London. But like many beloved homes, it's the feeling inside and the view *out* that are most important. The Botanist is a perfectly pleasant modern bar and dining room from which you can get ace views of the well-heeled people of Chelsea going about their daily shopping. Afternoon tea is a particular treat with dainty sandwiches and good scones and clotted cream. But lunch or dinner, when the bar is full of beautiful people, are pretty good too, with a standout Pear Tart Tatin.

Bluebird Café is a great meeting place, with tables on the terrace giving perfect ringside viewing of all the social interactions of a Chelsea weekend. The prices may reflect the chichi nature of the neighbourhood, but the Bluebird is one of the best places to meet, drink and hang a while in this neck of the woods.

The Bibendum Oyster Bar (*pictured*) is in a lavishly beautiful tiled building, formerly the headquarters of the French tyre company, Michelin. You cannot book, but can usually get a table for an impromptu light lunch, of seafood and salad, and if you are blessed by good weather the best table is outside by the flower stand, giving you a great view of all the action on the street. Alternatively, just wander the genteel streets with an ice cream from **Oddono's** (14 Bute St; tel: 020 7052 0732; map C5), which has 130 delicious flavours to choose from.

The Botanist, 7 Sloane Square; tel: 020 7730 0077; map E5
Bluebird Café, 350 King's Road; tel: 020 7559 1141; map C3
The Bibendum Oyster Bar, Michelin House, 81 Fulham Road; tel: 020 7251 0848; map D5

Step inside the Darwin Centre's **amazing high-tech Cocoon** and see science in action

When the Natural History Museum opened its £78 million extension, the Darwin Centre, in 2009, they did it with the express purpose of inspiring the next generation of naturalists and scientists. Merely housing their collections, and the people who study them, was not enough. They wanted museum-goers to get involved and be excited by the knowledge-gathering too. And they have achieved it brilliantly. The eight-storey glass-and-steel building has a weird white cocoon (it looks as if it's about to hatch a massive bug worthy of a scary sci-fi movie) at its public point of entry. You ride a glass lift to the top and then work your way down the Cocoon's white ramps looking at everything from specimens brought back by Darwin from his first exhibition on *The Beagle* in 1831 to the latest species of lichen or dust mite to be discovered. Educators are always talking about how knowledge is power, and you really feel the buzz of it as you wander round, interacting with glass screens, watching cases of bugs or birds or berries reveal their secrets as you press buttons, and get to observe, and interact with, the white-coated scientists as they go about their researches.

The Darwin Centre is a destination in its own right, but if you have time don't neglect the beautiful Victorian halls of its older sibling, **The Natural History Museum**. It has fantastic exhibits of dinosaurs and other marvellous creatures, including the dodo, and a full-size model of a blue whale. Right next door, the **Science Museum** with its many child-friendly interactive exhibits can also be an electrifying place.

The Darwin Centre, The Natural History Museum, Cromwell Road; tel: 020 7942 5000; www.nhm.ac.uk; daily 10am–5.50pm, booking required for timed slots; free; map C5
Science Museum, Exhibition Road; www.sciencemuseum.org.uk; daily 10am–6pm; free; map C6

Relish a **heavenly choir** in the ornate Italian Renaissance splendour of the **Brompton Oratory**

This flamboyant Baroque church is arguably London's most famous catholic church, and undoubtedly the most Roman as it is an almost exact imitation of the Church of the Gesù in Rome. The Oratory also has treasures from Italy scattered around it such as the giant statues of the Twelve Apostles in the nave, which were carved from Carrara marble by Giuseppe Mazzuoli in the 1680s and brought here from Siena's cathedral when the Oratory was completed in 1884. And the magnificent Lady Altar created for the Dominican church in Brescia in 1693.

The London Oratory, to give it its proper name, was the first Roman Catholic church to be built in England after the Reformation, and it still adheres to the rigid ritualised 'high' Catholicism popular in that day. Every Sunday there is a Mass sung in Latin, and while this marble-encrusted church is much admired for its architecture and elaborate painted ceiling, it is the music that's really made its name.

The Oratory has three choirs. The repertoire of the internationally renowned Choir of the London Oratory covers all periods of music from Gregorian chant to the present day, and the choir takes part in liturgies here most days. Then there is the boys-only London Oratory School Schola who perform at concerts around the city and sing at the Saturday 6pm Mass. Sweeter still is the junior choir, comprised of 8–16 year-olds from around the city, who you can catch practising after school most days of the week.

The Brompton Oratory, Brompton Road; tel: 020 7808 0900; www. bromptonorotary.com; map C6

Put your feet up in the Victoria & Albert Museum's delightful John Madejski Garden

Whatever you think of the vicissitudes of fashion, you'd have to admit that any museum that has a little black dress, as first conceived by Coco Chanel, in its permanent collection must be quite an interesting place. And the V&A is uniquely absorbing. Widely acclaimed as the greatest decorative arts museum in the world, it is also one of London's liveliest and most imaginative museums. However, there are 7 miles of galleries to traipse around and over 4.5 million objects – ceramics, furniture, fashion, glass, jewellery, photographs, sculpture, textiles, paintings – to marvel at, and the V&A is a notoriously complicated building to navigate, so pick up one of the free maps on your way in. Or resign yourself to the almost inevitable, and get a little lost. It's a wonderful place to be lost in. Finding your way out again is bound to introduce you to some object that had passed you by.

Another option is to 'cheat' and take a free one-hour tour (from the Meeting Point near Grand Entrance, every hour on the half hour from 10.30am to 3.30pm) to orient yourself. Otherwise wear flat shoes, and make sure you know where the **John Madejski Garden** is before you set out. This is the delightful courtyard where you can have a picnic, dip your throbbing toes in cool water, or simply rest awhile.

Between your calming interludes in the garden, consider venturing to: the **Fashion Gallery** (Room 40), for an overview of the British contribution to fashion since the 18th century, and a collection of corsetry through the ages that is sure to make you wince; the **British Galleries** (Rooms 52–58), devoted to British designers from 1500 to 1900 and full of beautiful diversions – among them the Great Bed of Ware, mentioned in Shakespeare's *Twelfth Night*; the **Japanese Gallery** (Room 44), which has a remarkable collection of ornate samurai armour; the **Exhibition**

Landscape Gallery (Room 87), with its breathtaking collection of British landscapes by Constable and Turner; the **Renaissance Sculpture Gallery** (Room 58), which includes Bernini's *Neptune with Triton*; and the **Cast Courts**, which have life-sized plaster models of ancient and medieval statuary and architecture including Michelangelo's *David*, and the front of Santiago de Compostela cathedral. The idea

was to allow artists unable to afford a 'grand tour' of Europe the chance to draw the treasures. It is to this day full of people sketching away. Don't be shy: bring a pad and have a doodle yourself.

Victoria & Albert Museum, Cromwell Rd; tel: 020 7942 2000; www.vam.ac.uk; daily 10am–5.45pm, Fri until 10pm; free; map C6

Get some **interior inspiration** at the **Design Centre Chelsea Harbour**

Ever secretly thought if only you had your life to live over again you'd be an interior designer and swish about with swatches of fabric, testing feather beds and choosing chandeliers? Well, the Design Centre Chelsea Harbour is the place to live out that fantasy. Once a best-kept secret open only to architects and decorators, it now welcomes the general public too. And very impressive it is too, with its three glass domes and immense black olive trees over which swoop graceful swans coming in to land. In the 83 showrooms you can find all the things you could need to create every style of home you have ever dreamed of. And even some you hadn't, like the lamps with duck feet in the Porta Romana shop, or the sideboard with the reclining sphinx on top at cabinet makers Stephen Ryan. You could even deck out that fantasy yacht here too (if walking round the harbour outside has given you boat envy). More prosaically you could just pick up some colour charts if you are thinking of repainting the kitchen, find out who makes the deepest sofa or the plushest carpet or treat yourself to a new bedside lamp, cushion, tea cup or bath mat.

The **Design Café** in the North Dome has salads, sandwiches and snacks in suitably designery surroundings or there's the nearby **Lots Road Pub and Dining Rooms** for a nice laidback Bloody Mary, Sunday lunch or bar snack.

The Design Centre, Chelsea Harbour; tel: 020 7225 9166; www.designcentre chelseaharbour.co.uk; Mon-Fri 9am-5.30pm; map B1

Attend a **concert in the Royal Albert Hall** – one of the world's most elegant auditoriums

The Royal Albert Hall is not quite the thing of magnificent beauty originally planned by Prince Albert, Queen Victoria's consort. He wanted a hall that seated 30,000, but his untimely death from typhoid meant that a large part of the funds (that had been donated by the public, his wife's loyal subjects) were diverted to creating his memorial statue. A gilded statue of Albert now sits in his memorial facing the Royal Albert Hall in Kensington Gardens, and his architects were left behind to carry on with the domed, round concert hall inspired by the Roman amphitheatres. But if Albert could look down on it now, it's unlikely he'd be disappointed with its reduction in size; it was scaled down to seat 7,000. He would almost certainly be delighted with the breadth of its reach – Wagner, Verdi and Elgar conducted the first UK performance of their own works here, and nearly every major classical solo artist and leading orchestra has performed at the Hall, as have many light entertainment, pop and rock artists including Frank Sinatra, Liza Minnelli, Jimi Hendrix, The Beatles, Elton John, Jay Z, Kaiser Chiefs and the Killers. But the hall is best known for the summer Proms, a series of BBC-sponsored classical concerts which provide a rich diet of affordable music.

Royal Albert Hall, Kensington Gore; tel: 0845 401 5045; www.royalalberthall. com; map B7

Strike a pose in the **sculpture garden** of the **Serpentine Gallery**

In the south-eastern corner of Kensington Gardens The Serpentine Gallery is a dynamic exhibition space for contemporary art, much-loved by Londoners. Each summer, the gallery gets to double in size and add another building, thanks to the summer pavilion project in which it commissions a famous international architect who has not, as yet, built in Britain, to create a 'temporary wing'. The pavilion stands from June to September and passers-by can whiz through it on their morning jog or have impromptu picnics in it, or just stop and admire it. The intent is to make contemporary architecture accessible, without dumbing it down. It lets you get up close and touch it.

The other exceptional feature of the Serpentine Gallery is the sculpture garden on the lawn surrounding it, which includes the tribute to Princess Diana (*see box below*), the gallery's former patron. This work, by poet and artist Ian Hamilton Finlay, is made up of eight benches, a tree-plaque, and a carved stone circle.

Serpentine Gallery, Kensington Gardens; tel: 020 7402 6075; www. serpentinegallery.org; daily 10am–6pm, free; map C7

MEMORIALS TO 'LADY DI'
If you are in the mood to pay tribute to 'the people's princess' there is: **Diana, Princess of Wales Memorial Fountain** (map C7) where you can dip your toes in cool flowing water; and **Diana, Princess of Wales Memorial Playground** (map A8) which, with its sand pits, pirate ship, teepees and tree houses, is very much fun. **Kensington Palace** (www.hrp.org.uk/KensingtonPalace; map A7) has a display of the gowns that she wore on state occasions. **Diana Princess of Wales, Memorial Walk** (www.royalparks.org.uk/tourists) is for the more energetic; this 7-mile walk is easy to follow thanks to the 90 plaques set in the ground, and takes in all the London buildings and places associated with Prince William and Harry's mum.

Take **afternoon tea** in the courtly splendour of **the Orangery**, **Kensington Palace**

Kensington Palace was initially a country house adapted for royal use by Sir Christopher Wren. It housed the courts of William II, Queen Anne, George I and George II, and was *the* London Palace until it was usurped by the bigger, flashier, Buckingham Palace. More recently it was a much-loved home to the late Princesses Margaret and Diana. Whether you opt to tour the house or not, you would be missing a treat if you didn't have breakfast, lunch or tea in the Orangery, a magnificent 18th-century building. The Orangery has a glorious setting inside the Palace grounds, giving you time and space to soak up the quintessentially English atmosphere and the lovely views of both the palace and the sunken gardens. Formidable white Corinthian pillars and marble statues lend the room a certain grandeur, while the piles of tempting own-made cakes can almost make you feel at home. The signature Orangery cake has a devoted following and is subject of much recipe guessing. A contender for best slice of London cake, it has a hit of sunny orange glow in every bite.

If, however, you find yourself in need of picking up or cooling down again after your visit to the Orangery, consider a quick detour to **Kensington Square Kitchen** (9 Kensington Square; tel: 020 7938 2598; map A6) for a very good cup of coffee.

The Orangery, Kensington Palace, Kensington Gardens; tel: 020 7376 0239; www.hrp.org.uk; daily, Mar–Oct 10am–6pm, Nov–Feb 10am–5pm; map A8

Make like Charles Saatchi and **collect art**, even if it is just on a T-shirt, at the **Saatchi Gallery**

British critics have almost to a man (and woman) been snooty about the Saatchi Gallery, calling it a study in bland. But to the average gallery-goer, it is actually a really nice place to look at art. Housed in the grand, 70,000 square feet of what was formerly the Duke of York's Barracks, the Saatchi has no rope barriers, the work is given lots of space, and the lighting is good. The walls are an unvarying shade of cream, the floors are uniform expanses of Danish pine and there are plenty of places to sit. However, and this would really get the critics in a snit, one of the major reasons to visit the Saatchi is the shop. They have a fantastic selection of art T-shirts and exciting contemporary jewellery. There is also a café with an outdoor terrace and some really good salads, soups and light lunches. If, however, you feel beholden to get involved with the art, be sure to visit the online gallery where you can put your work on show to the thousands of visitors a day. Those who have always said modern art was so simple, a child of five could do it, may be given pause for thought by this exercise.

The Saatchi Gallery, Duke of York's HQ, King's Road; tel: 020 7811 3085; www. saatchi-gallery.co.uk; daily 10am–6pm; free admission to all shows; map E4

Lift your spirits in the **Blue Bar at the Berkeley Hotel** and other plush haunts

It is hard to say exactly why the **Blue Bar at the Berkeley Hotel** is so gorgeous. Is it the way it's painted the perfect shade of peregrine blue so beloved of English country homes? Is it the friendly staff who always seem to be at beckoning distance without seeming to hover or be ingratiating? Could it be the inventive list of cocktails including the showy Manhattan that comes fizzing with dry ice? Or the extreme care with which your drinks are prepared? Or the delicious free little dishes of nuts or biscuits that arrive without being requested? Whatever it is, this is the perfect place for a quiet tête-a-tête or a little discreet celebrity-watching.

Despite its name, the **Tini Bar** has a massive bar specialising in Martinis, Negroni and other Italian cocktail classics. There is a distinctly '80s feel about the place, but that is actually very 'now'. So put on your best high-shouldered dress or suit and: enjoy!

At first glance **Bar 190** looks like your average hotel bar, but at second glance there's something very rock 'n' roll about it. Perhaps that is because it was the setting of the Rolling Stones film *Beggars*

Banquet. Or more likely, it's because it is the scene of many an after-party for musicians, and their hangers-on, who have performed at the Royal Albert Hall.

Blue Bar at the Berkeley Hotel, Wilton Place; tel: 020 7235 6000; map E7
Tini Bar, 87–89 Walton Street; tel: 020 7589 8558; map D5
Bar 190, The Gore Hotel, 190 Kensington Gate; tel: 020 7584 6601; map B6

A **day of luxury** and relaxation at the **Mandarin Oriental Spa**

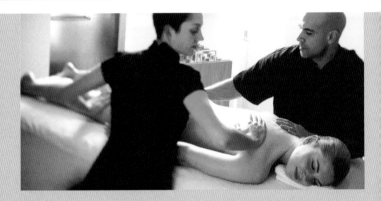

The mood at the Mandarin Oriental Spa is as calm and Zen as the countenance of a Buddhist monk. It is all tea lights, fresh orchids, rainforest-hot steam rooms and chiming Tibetan cymbals (they mark the beginning and end of each treatment). Voices are hushed and black-robed therapists discreetly move through the dark granite rooms. Most of the treatments are Eastern in origin, focusing on chakras and with names like Ayurvedic Holistic Body Treatment, Oriental Head Massage, and Detoxifying Sea of Senses. There is a two-hour time-slot minimum, and the idea is that your therapist will tailor a 'ritual' to meet your needs (and fit your wallet) during that time. Between times you can sip juice or a herbal tea in the Zen Relaxation Area with colour therapy lights to further soothe your nerves, all ensuring that when you come out you will feel as smooth, burnished and golden as a statue of the Buddha.

The Spa at Mandarin Oriental, 66 Knightsbridge; tel: 020 7838 9888; www. mandarinoriental.com; map E7

GREAT SPA EXPERIENCES IN LONDON
The Berkeley Spa (Wilton Place; tel: 020 7235 6000; map E7) is arguably London's most glamorous spa, with its swimming pool overlooking Hyde Park and fabulous treatments. **Bliss London** (60 Sloane Ave; tel: 020 7584 3888; map D5) for a beauteous slice of New York life. **Agua at the Sanderson** (50 Berners St; tel: 020 7300 1414; map p.84, B2) for the most luxurious futurist feel.

Check out the year-round **herb and flower show** at **Chelsea Physic Garden**

Step inside the walls of the Chelsea Physic Garden and three things happen in quick succession: the noise of the main road and the city disappears, your senses are assailed by the tangled fragrances of many plants and herbs, and you realise that, pretty as it is, this is no ordinary garden. No, this is a garden with a purpose (and it's not to be pretty). Founded in 1673 as a botanical education centre, the plants grown here have changed the course of nations – rubber plants from here went to Malaysia, and tea trees (thanks to seeds gathered in China) went to India. The garden has also changed lives: they grow around 4,000 different plants, including opium poppies, and Pacific Yew, the bark of which contains taxol, an effective drug used in the treatment of breast cancer. Perhaps less impressively, the Chelsea Physic Garden also boasts Britain's largest olive tree and the world's northernmost outdoor grapefruit tree. Children seem particularly to love the scary collection of carnivorous plants in one of the greenhouses.

There is a café, open from Wednesday to Sunday, serving good food. On a nice day you can carry your cups of tea out into the garden, or bring a picnic and sit on one of the many benches scattered throughout this fragrant haven.

Chelsea Physic Garden, 66 Royal Hospital Road; tel: 020 7352 5646; www.chelseaphysicgarden.co.uk; Apr–Oct Wed–Fri, Sun noon–5pm; map D3

155

Village London

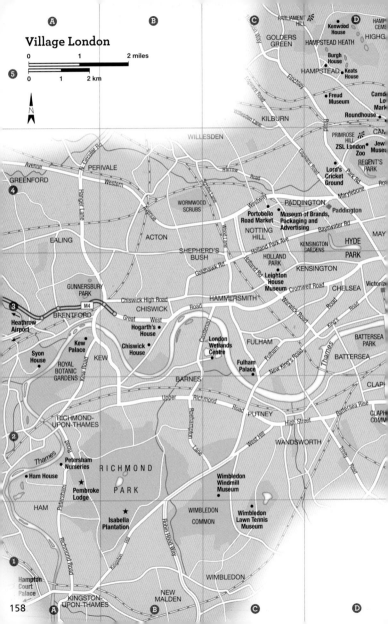

Village London

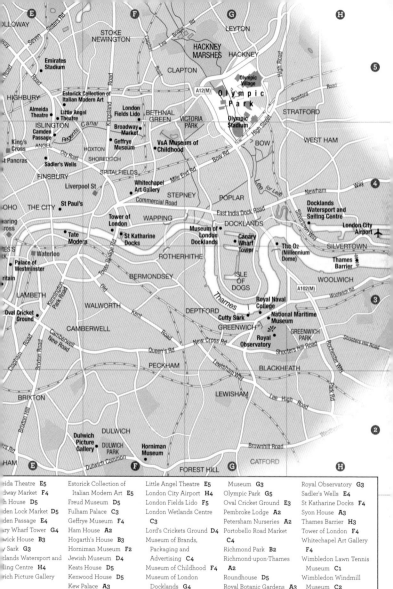

Ride the tube to **Notting Hill** for its antiques and chic boutiques, then relax in the **Holland Park** oasis

Walking around **Notting Hill** (map C4; tube: Ladbroke Grove, Notting Hill Gate) with its chichi shops, cool bars and trendy, well-heeled residents, you would never guess that, as recently as the 1960s, this was one of London's most poverty-stricken areas. Or that, in the 1950s it gave rise to Britain's first race riots when white Teddy boys clashed with incoming Caribbean residents. That is all in the past, although the Caribbean tradition is still proudly celebrated annually with the Notting Hill Carnival (August bank holiday weekend).

The two biggest attractions are **Portobello Road** (www.portobelloroad.co.uk) and Holland Park. The former bursts into life as an antiques market on Saturday (8am–5pm), but week-round has many fantastic little antique shops and boutiques for vintage (and vintage-inspired) clothes such as **Mensah** (291). There are also some great cafés, including **Café Garcia** (246) where the gazpacho is as good as any you'll find in Spain. Be sure to wander down **All Saints Road** for offbeat shops and the organic pub, **The Pelican** (45).

The Museum of Brands, Packaging and Advertising (2 Colville Mews, Lonsdale Rd, tel: 020 7908 0880; www.museumof brands.com) is a fascinating small museum devoted to social ephemera where you can take a trip down memory lane and reconnect with all the long-forgotten packaging of your favourite childhood treats.

Holland Park (map C3; tube: Holland Park) is a grand oasis of green space where you really feel you are in the countryside. At its southern end, the **Leighton House Museum** (12 Holland Park Rd; tel: 020 7602 3316; www.rbkc.gov.uk) is a must for anyone interested in Victorian art, while the **Orangery Gallery** and tea rooms are a must for anyone interested in a good cup of tea in a beautiful setting.

Immerse yourself in the **Camden market and music scene**, then walk the **canal path to Regent's Park**

With a whopping 10 million visitors a year, **Camden Market** (map D5; tube: Camden Town, Chalk Farm) is one of London's biggest attractions, a huge sprawl of six markets from Camden to Chalk Farm. And quantity has perhaps brought with it a dilution of quality, but there are still some great finds among the tat, including creative clothing for goths, rockabillies and burlesque artistes at **Black Rose** (Shop 26 Stables Market), excellent vintage at **A Dandy in Aspic** (Unit D13 Horse Tunnel Market), and ceramic art at **Painted Earth** (Arch 65 The Catacombs, Stables Market).

But there's a lot more to the neighbourhood than its market. Camden has long been the spiritual home of London's music scene. Among the best venues are: **The Roundhouse** (Chalk Farm Rd) with its eclectic mix of concerts and theatre, **Barfly** (49 Chalk Farm Rd), which is credited with having launched loads of successful bands, including The Strokes and Coldplay, and the **Jazz Café** (5 Parkway), which, despite its name, is a top venue for soul and R&B.

Some of London's most valuable property is in backstreet Camden, and a stroll down the Regent's Canal allows you to peek into some very grand gardens indeed. If you follow the canal heading west from the market, you will be in **Regent's Park** (map D4) within about 15 minutes. The park is another huge draw with its gently sloping lawns, rose gardens, football and softball pitches, and the **ZSL London Zoo** (tel: 020 7722 3333; www.zsl.org).

Cross Prince Albert Road, and you are in genteel **Primrose Hill** park (map D4). The energetic should climb the hill for its beautiful views back down over the whole city, and explore **Regent's Park Road**, which is lined with chichi shops and great cafés.

Shop and socialise in elegant **Islington**, one of the capital's favourite **drinking and dining** spots

Now considered fairly central, **Islington** (map E4/5; tube: Angel) was built in the 19th century as one of London's first suburbs, and has some of the city's most elegant late Georgian and early Victorian squares including the neo-Gothic **Lonsdale Square** which is definitely worth a detour with its beautiful gardens in the centre.

Upper Street, which acts as the area's main thoroughfare, is one of London's better high streets, with lots of interesting independent shops among the more obvious chain names. Antique lovers throng to **Camden Passage** on Wednesdays and Saturdays for the market. There's a fantastic independent cinema, **Screen on the Green** (83), and great cafés, like the **Euphorium Bakery** (202) for coffee, sandwiches and amazing tarts, **Ottolenghi** (287) for delicious Middle Eastern-influenced Mediterranean dishes, or **Gallipolli Café Bistro** (102) where you can while away a lazy afternoon eating meze in a party atmosphere.

Islington is also the capital's alternative theatre land, with more stage space per capita than any other part of London. **Sadler's Wells** (Rosebery Ave; tel: 020 7863 8198; www.sadlers wells.com) is London's 'dance

house'. **The King's Head** (115 Upper Street; 020 7226 8561; www.kingsheadtheatre.org) was the first pub theatre opened since Shakespeare's day and has launched the careers of Hugh Grant and Alan Rickman. There is also the **Almeida** (Almeida St; tel: 020 7226 7432; www. almeida.co.uk), one of London's most innovative small theatres, which has a great restaurant and bar attached, and the **Little Angel Theatre** (14 Dagmar Passage; tel: 020 7359 8581; www. littleangeltheatre.com), where children are mesmerised by amazing puppet shows.

Discover two illuminating **East End museums** and take a riverside walk through the **Docklands**

The term 'East End' refers to the area extending out north and east from the old walled City of London. To Londoners, 'East End' conjures up images of chirpy cockneys, gritty dockland locations and associations with poverty and immigration. But that is far from the whole story, and the entire area is now benefiting from regeneration and hipness radiating outwards from Hoxton and Shoreditch (p.164). The biggest news in the East End is the 2012 Olympics. An army of construction workers has been beavering away to erect the new **Olympic Park** (map G5) in Stratford, which will change the face of this traditionally deprived part of town. But there will be no access to the sporting stadia (including Zaha Hadid's splendid Aquatic Centre) until after the opening of the Games.

Two East End museums worth an excursion are the **V&A Museum of Childhood** (Cambridge Heath Rd; tel: 020 8983 5200; tube: Bethnal Green; map F4) a family favourite, with lots of activities for kids, a big comfortable café and some amusing exhibits; and the **Museum of London Docklands** (West India Quay, Canary Wharf; tel: 020 7001 9844; www. museumindocklands.org.uk; tube: Canary Wharf; map G4), which studies the fascinating history of what was once the world's largest port. From here you can take a walk through the modern Docklands area along the Thames Path, heading for **The Narrow Street Pub and Dining Room** (44 Narrow St; DLR: Limehouse) just after the Limehouse Basin, which has an expansive terrace overlooking the river.

Survey the **contemporary art scene**, then join the
Shoreditch and Hoxton lounge lizards

The postcodes E1 and E2 have the highest concentration of artists in Europe, and are a thriving cultural quarter. Many people come for the galleries, but most flock here for the drinking, the eating and the general vibe. **Shoreditch and Hoxton** (map F4) are great to just wander around seeing where you end up. Here's a sample of places to get you started.

GALLERIES
Victoria Miro (16 Wharf Rd; tel: 020 7336 8109), an elegantly converted warehouse in which to see Peter Doig, Chris Ofili and Grayson Perry. **Parasol Unit** (14 Wharf Rd; tel: 020 7490 7373) is a swanky, not-for-profit space with an artist-in-residence scheme and first-rate exhibitions. **White Cube** (48 Hoxton Square; tel: 020 7930 5373) is an essential destination for artists famous or about-to-be. **Store** (27 Hoxton St; tel: 020 7729 8171) also shows rising stars. **Rivington Place** (tel: 020 7749 1240) public gallery has a permanent collection of international contemporary art. **Rocket** (Tea Building, 56 Shoreditch High St; tel: 020 7729 7594) exhibits well-known photographers. Finish your gallery

tour by walking down Redchurch Street where you will find many smaller galleries such as **The Outside World** (44) and a fantastic old-style London pub **The Owl & the Pussycat** (34), and...

CAFES, BARS, RESTAURANTS
... **Macondo** (Unit 2a, 8–9 Hoxton Square) for coffee, cake and snacks. **Yelo** (8–9 Hoxton Square) – great Thai food upstairs, trendy bar downstairs. **The Breakfast Club** (2–4 Rufus St) for all-day fry-ups. **Les Trois Garcons** (1 Club Row) is a great restaurant upstairs from **Loungelovers,** a cool cocktail bar. Arguably London's best takeaway cup of

coffee can be had from **Prufrock Coffee**, tucked inside menswear store **Present** (140 Shoreditch High St). Down the Kingsland Road is the way to go for fantastic cheap Vietnamese food.

A MUSEUM AND A MARKET

While here, visit **The Geffrye Museum** (136 Kingsland Rd; tel: 020 7739 9893; www.geffrye-museum.org), a series of rooms decorated in all the most popular styles from 1600 to the present day, set out in elegant 18th-century almshouses surrounded by period gardens.

If you are in the area on a Saturday, try **Broadway Market** (London Fields), a great little market for vintage clothes, food and authentic London bustle.

The nearest tube for Shoreditch is Liverpool Street and for Hoxton it is Old Street. Or Dalston Junction on the new East London Line overland trains is handy for both.

Retreat to the **royal gardens of Kew and Richmond** where the banks of the Thames turn rural

Ever wondered what else the architects of the London Eye have done for London? Well hop on board the first boat, bus or train to Kew and see the stairway to heaven they've built at **Kew Gardens** (map A3; tube/train: Kew Gardens). The Rhizotron and Xstrata Treetop Walkway takes you 60ft up in the air to stroll among tree tops. It's breathtaking, as is the rest of the Royal Botanic Gardens; the largest living plant collection in the world where you can take tea in the Orangery, and delight at the towering tropical plants of the Palm House (*pictured*).

Kew is approximately 6 miles from central London, and here the Thames is a tamer, prettier, almost bucolic thing, making this one of the best places for a river walk. The 3-mile stretch between Kew Bridge and Richmond Bridge allows you to look in the gardens, and the Old Deer Park and gives beautiful views across the river.

Richmond-upon-Thames (map A2; tube/train: Richmond) is a lovely old town within greater London, with royal connections going back centuries, and is still a wealthy district with some handsome palaces and parks to explore. On the top of Richmond Hill is the largest city park in Europe, **Richmond Park** – 12 square miles of undulating meadows, and coppiced woodland full of deer which roam freely and are remarkably friendly, much to the delight of visiting children.

Back down the hill, if you continue along the towpath beyond Richmond Bridge for a mile you reach **Ham House** (tel: 020 8940 0735), a remarkably well-preserved 17th-century house with spectacular gardens and statuary.

Stroll, swim or skate on **Hampstead Heath** and go on the trail of its illustrious former residents

Between the exclusive villages of Hampstead and Highgate is the marvellous verdant sprawl of **Hampstead Heath** (map D5; tube: Hampstead) – 320 hectares of woodlands, hills and ponds. The top of **Parliament Hill** has benches conveniently placed to sit and gaze out over the panorama of London or the kite flyers and dog walkers all around. Sporty types should head for one of the three **bathing ponds** – men's, women's or mixed – for a dip. And arty types should go to **Kenwood House** (tel: 020 8348 1286; www.english-heritage. org.uk; tube Archway/Golder's Green, then 210 bus), a neoclassical mansion that has Henry Moore and Barbara Hepworth statues in its grounds, and a summer programme of open-air concerts.

Over the years, Hampstead was known as an area for intellectuals, and there are house museums to pay tribute to its most illustrious former residents. At the **Freud Museum** (20 Maresfield Gardens; tel: 020 7435 2002; www.freud. org.uk; tube: Finchley Road) you can see the great analyst's couch, though not sit on it. **Keat's House** (Keats Grove; tel: 020 7435 2062; www.keatshouse.cityoflondon. gov.uk; tube: Hampstead Heath) is the elegant Regency villa where Keats wrote odes and fell in love with his neighbour, Fanny Brawne. And **Karl Marx** is laid to rest in **Highgate Cemetery** (tube: Highgate) – 20 wild and atmospheric hectares full of dramatic and ornate Victorian graves and sombre tombs.

Both Highgate and Hampstead villages are dotted with lovely old pubs, including the allegedly haunted **Spaniards Inn** (Spaniards Road), and **The Flask** (Highgate West Hill), which has a big front garden and good Sunday lunches.

Be seduced by two handsome south London suburbs – historic Greenwich and leafy Dulwich

The importance of **Greenwich** (DLR/train: Greenwich; map G3) stretches further back in time than the Middle Ages. On the south bank of the Thames, the ancient village was the gateway between London and the Channel ports. By the 18th century the combination of Britain's wealth, maritime power and scientific learning had blessed Greenwich with the most beautiful ensemble of buildings in the British Isles.

The most spectacular way to visit Greenwich is by boat (www.dlrlondon.co.uk or www. thamesriverservices.co.uk). This way you can begin your Greenwich trip at the riverfront, gazing at the Baroque splendour of the raised colonnades and twin domes of Sir Christopher Wren's **Royal Naval College** framing the elegant simplicity of the **Queen's House**, designed by Inigo Jones in 1616. Next door, the **National Maritime Museum** (www.nmm. ac.uk; tel: 020 8858 4422) displays an unrivalled collection of maritime art and artefacts. Its 16 galleries are set around Neptune Courtyard, a spectacular space, spanned by a glass roof. The oldest of England's royal parks, the vast and glorious **Greenwich Park** dates from 1433, when the Duke of Gloucester, King Henry V's brother, created it.

Walk up the hill from the museum and you reach its most famous building, the **Royal Observatory** (www.rog.nmm.ac.uk;

tel: 020 8858 4422) Here you can stand astride the **Prime Meridian line**, a brass rail set in concrete that allows you to have one foot in the western hemisphere and the other in the eastern.

The heart of Greenwich lies just west of the park. Here you'll find the clipper ship the **Cutty Sark**, currently being restored after a fire in 2007, Hawksmoor's **St Alfege's Church**, and **Greenwich Market** (Wed–Sun), full of little arts and crafts and food stalls.

Royal Hill is a lovely Georgian street with a gorgeous old pub,

Richard I (52 Royal Hill), at one end and a very hip gastro-pub, **The Hill**, at the other.

Another historic south London suburb, often overlooked, **Dulwich** is also packed with interesting and historic places. **Dulwich Park** (College Road) has magnificent old oak trees and a large lake. **The Dulwich Picture Gallery** (7 Gallery Road; www.dulwichpicturegallery.org.uk; tel: 020 8693 4786; train: West Dulwich) has a superb collection of Baroque paintings. **The Horniman Museum** (100 London Road; www.horniman.ac.uk; tel: 020 8699 1872; train: Forest Hill) is a truly eccentric museum with an aquarium and a small children's zoo, all of which is set in a hilly park.

hotels

The hotels on offer in London reflect the full scope of the city – from the famously grand and formal, represented by Claridges, right down to the most imaginative, tiny and informal sort of place, such as the pop-up hotel occasionally operated by the Visit London tourist board in a beautifully restored airstream caravan parked near to one of London's sights and attractions.

Time was London was all about the very grand hotel or the cheap B&B depending on your income, with only bland expense-account business hotels occupying the middle market. But in the past couple of decades there's been a positive explosion of boutique hotels – characterful, charming and beautifully designed hotels that make a lot of the peculiarly London buildings and locations they are in – whether it be a town house (Hazlitt's), a hospital (Covent Garden and Charlotte Street hotels) or an office block (St Martin's Lane).

With the honourable exception of Mayfair, home of the exclusive, high-luxury and very expensive hotel, you cannot necessarily predict a hotel's style or expense by its location. Thus in the very posh area of Kensington, for example, you get the plush, stately home hotel next to the no-frills bed and breakfast. And in trendy Hoxton you get the rough-at-the-edges hostelry sharing postal codes with swanky establishments.

HOTEL PRICES
Price for an average room in high season, including breakfast

££££ over £300
£££ £200–300
££ £125–200
£ under £125

The lap of luxury

Claridges
🟦 Mayfair

49 Brook Street; tel: 020 7629 8860; www.claridges.co.uk; map p.25 C4; ££££

In the heart of Mayfair, Claridges is the epitome of the grand English hotel. It opened in 1854 and has been so favoured by royal and aristocratic families that it's often referred to as 'an extension of Buckingham Palace'. The reception rooms are Art Deco, and the bedrooms are English country chintz with welcome modern touches.

The Lanesborough
🟦 Belgravia

Hyde Park Corner; tel: 020 7259 5599; www.lanesborough.co.uk; map p.66 A3; ££££

Want to pretend that you are nobility residing in a great house? The Lanesborough is your place. Built as the country home of the Viscount Lanesborough, it positively reeks grandeur, and there are butlers assigned to each room to act as your 'downstairs' staff.

Mandarin Oriental, Hyde Park
🟦 Kensington

66 Knightsbridge; tel: 020 7235 2000; www.mandarinoriental.com; map p.140 E7; ££££

This sumptuous hotel overlooking Hyde Park exudes elegance and offers impeccable service. Be pampered in its luxurious spa (p.154), have a sophisticated drink at the bar, or experience the 'molecular gastronomy' of celebrity chef Heston Blumenthal (due to open a restaurant in late 2010).

History and tradition

Hazlitt's
Soho
6 Frith Street; tel: 020 7434 1771; www.
hazlittshotel.com; map p. 46 D5; £££
Hazlitt's is in a group of 18th-century
town houses, one of which was
originally home to essayist William
Hazlitt. It is still favoured by writers,
including Bill Bryson, for its charm,
period features – claw-footed baths,
library full of first-edition manuscripts
– and modern conveniences –
broadband, TV, and in-room massages.

The Gore Hotel
Kensington
189 Queen's Gate; tel: 020 7584 6601;
www.gorehotel.com; map p.140 B6; £££
Close to the Albert Hall, The Gore
is ideally located for Hyde Park, the
Natural History and the Victoria
and Albert museums. And as such is
perfect for art-loving traditionalists.
A grand staircase lined with ornate
mirrors leads up to cosy, individually
decorated bedrooms full of antiques
and fine paintings.

Browns Hotel
Mayfair
33 Albemarle Street; tel 020 7493 6020;
www.brownshotel.com; map p.24 C5; ££££
Founded by James Brown, a former
manservant to Lord Byron, this town-
house hotel certainly knows about
discreet service and how to make
you feel really cared for. Some of the
rooms have four-poster beds and all
have antique washbasins. Browns is
also famous for its quintessentially
English afternoon tea.

The Cadogan
Chelsea
75 Sloane Street; tel 020 7235 7141; www.
cadogan.com; map p.140 E6; £££
A whiff of scandal once permeated the
elegant corridors of this Edwardian-
style hotel (Oscar Wilde was arrested
here in 1895 and the future Edward VII
was entertained by his mistress Lily
Langtry here). Today, it is all discretion
and quiet charm. Harrods and Harvey
Nichols are a short walk away.

In the centre of it all

The Langham Hotel
■ Marylebone

1C Portland Place; tel: 020 3174 0200;
www.london.langhamhotels.co.uk;
map p.24 D6; ££££

Tucked away at the top of Regent
Street, a short walk from Oxford
Circus, the elegant Langham Hotel
is fabulously well placed for the West
End. The Langham has recently
enjoyed an £80 million face-lift, which
transformed the Artesian Bar into one
of London's coolest hotel bars.

Charlotte Street Hotel
■ Fitzrovia

5 Charlotte Street; tel: 020 7806 2000;
www.firmdale.com; map p.84 C2; ££££

Charlotte Street is the smartest
street north of Oxford Street, and the
eponymous hotel is one of the chicest
boutique hotels in London. Bedrooms
are individually designed in a country-
house style, with big bathrooms. There
is also a lovely sitting room with
roaring fire and a private cinema.

Covent Garden Hotel
■ Covent Garden

10 Monmouth Street; tel: 020 7806 1000;
www.firmdale.com; map p.47 H3; ££££

One of London's most charming
boutique hotels, the Covent Garden,
is in the Seven Dials, the West End's
hippest shopping neighbourhood.
It's also very well placed for theatres
and the Royal Opera House. This
former hospital has a dramatic
stone staircase, and soundproofed
bedrooms.

Montagu Place
Marylebone

2 Montagu Place; tel: 020 7467 2777; www.montagu-place.co.uk; map p.24 A6; ££

The sleek modern decor of Montagu Place chimes very well with the Georgian town house in which it is set. The quiet residential square is a minute away from the frantic activity of Oxford Street. There are three grades of bedroom – comfy, fancy and swanky – each of which has all mod cons.

Radisson Edwardian Berkshire
Marylebone

350 Oxford Street; tel: 020 7629 7474; www.radissonedwardian.com/berkshire; map p.24 C5; ££

This hotel is on Oxford Street, London's busiest shopping area, and a stone's throw from Marylebone High Street, so couldn't be better placed for the West End shops if it tried. And inside is a sleek, clubby and quiet oasis with leather sofas and a decent restaurant, the Ascot.

St Martin's Lane
Covent Garden

45 St Martin's Lane; tel: 020 7300 5500; www.stmartinslane.com; map p.47 E3; ££££

Once a nondescript office block, this chic minimalist hotel is ideally placed for shopping, theatre and the national galleries. The bar was the height of hip when it opened in the 1990s, and has not lost any of its allure. The stark white rooms are cool too – you can paint them any colour you want with the full-spectrum lighting.

Cheap and cheerful

The Arosfa Hotel
Bloomsbury

83 Gower Street; tel: 020 7636 2115; www. arosfalondon.com; map p.84 C3; £

Bang in the middle of Bloomsbury, this friendly, family-run hotel is in a lovely Georgian terraced house, once home to the Pre-Raphaelite painter, Millais. Despite being Welsh-owned (arosfa is Welsh for 'a place to stay'), the reception area has a London meets Hollywood feel. The bedrooms are small, but clean and smart, and all have flat-screen TVs.

myhotel Bloomsbury
Bloomsbury

11–13 Bayley Street, Bedford Square, London; tel: 020 3004 6000; www.Myhotels. com/Bloomsbury; map p.84 C3; ££

Tucked in a calm little oasis where Tottenham Court Road meets Oxford Street, this boutique hotel is all muted colours and crisp lines. The bedrooms are uncluttered but comfortable. The Mybar/café, which serves light meals and meze, is a popular meeting place for people who work and play in the area.

The Hoxton Hotel
Hoxton

81 Great Eastern Street; tel: 020 7550 1000; www.hoxtonhotels.com; map p.103 F5; ££

Billed as 'the luxury budget hotel', the Hoxton has the highest-quality Egyptian cotton sheets, but limited room service, and you get a free Pret a Manger breakfast outside your door in the morning (the people behind the popular sandwich chain run the Hoxton). It is on a very busy road, but many rooms overlook a quiet square.

B+B Belgravia
Belgravia

64–66 Ebury Street; tel: 020 7259 8570; www.bb-belgravia; map p.66 B1; £

This Georgian town-house B&B, on a quiet tree-lined street near Victoria Station, has won several awards from the London tourist board. The building has a Georgian facade, but inside it is very chic and contemporary and there is a cool open kitchen with views over a lovely garden, where the friendly staff will cook you a hot breakfast to order.

myhotel Chelsea
Chelsea

35 Ixworth Place; tel: 020 7225 7500; www. myhotels.com; map p.141 D4; ££

Like its bigger sister, Myhotel Bloomsbury, this 45-room hotel lies just out of the throng, two minutes' walk from Brompton Cross. It has a more luxurious feel with cashmere bed throws, plasma-screen TVs, and Aveda bathroom products. The guest-only conservatory has big sofas and stacks of DVDs, novels and board games.

Designer chic

Andaz
The City
40 Liverpool Street; tel: 020 7618 7000;
www.london.liverpoolstreet.andaz.hyatt.
com; map p.103 F3; £££
Behind the glorious Victorian exterior
of Andaz, formerly the Great Eastern
Hotel, its new owners, Hyatt, have
orchestrated a clever marriage
between the cutting-edge design of
neighbouring Shoreditch and Hoxton
and an allegiance to old-fashioned
British pomp and circumstance.

The Zetter
Clerkenwell
86–88 Clerkenwell Road; tel: 020 7324 4444;
www.thezetter.com; map p.102 C5; ££
With the huge bright pink letter Z
above the front door, the Zetter oozes
designer cool even before you step
inside. And the more you know, the
cooler it seems: the bottled water
comes from the Zetter's own well; it
has a cool restaurant; and it's on the
doorstep of all the trendy clubs and
bars of Clerkenwell and Smithfield.

The Boundary
Shoreditch
2–4 Boundary St; tel: 020 7729 1051; www.
theboundary.co.uk; map p.103 G5; £££
Each bedroom in this seriously stylish
hotel from Sir Terence Conran is named
after a designer or design movement
– Eames, van der Rohe, Bauhaus, etc.
It also has a great restaurant, cool café
and a fantastic roof terrace. The only
drawback is the location on the borders
of Shoreditch which some find slightly
too dark and grungy.

The Sanderson
Fitzrovia
50 Berners Street, London; tel: 020 7300
1400; www.sandersonlondon.com;
map p.84 B2; £££
A landmark modernist 1950s building
has been turned into a de luxe modern
dreamworld by Philippe Starck. There's
a beautiful calm indoor courtyard, an
award-winning spa (see p.154), and each
room is a sensual romantic retreat – the
bathroom is a glass box swathed in
layers of sheer fabric.

Family friendly

Renaissance London Chancery Court Hotel
Holborn

252 High Holborn; tel: 020 7829 9888; www.marriott.co.uk; map p.85 F2; £££

This business hotel is also welcoming to families. Mum will be happy with the Penhaligons goodies in the bathroom, dad may appreciate the special 'duck package' which includes a tour of the city on amphibious vehicles, and the kids will love their special duck passports and toys.

Base2Stay
Kensington

25 Courtfield Gardens; tel: 0845 262 8000; www.base2stay.com; map p.140 A5; £

With its grand, white facade and smart black and cream reception, Base2Stay looks like a classic boutique hotel. Except this is a no-frills kind of a place – there's no bar, restaurant or gym – which is great for families. Each double room comes with kichenette so you can make your kids' tea before settling them into their bunk beds or cots.

The Soho Hotel
Soho

4 Richmond Mews; tel: 020 7559 3000; www.firmdale.com; map p.46 C4; £££

Kids love it here from the moment they see the ten-foot fat cat sculpture and oversized plant pots in the lobby. They are also made to feel welcome in this modern luxury lair, and there is a kids' menu on room service and in the restaurant.

Premier Inn County Hall
Southbank

Belvedere Road; tel: 0870 238 3300; www.premieriinn.com; map p.122 A3; ££

This clean, efficient hotel is right by the London Eye so very well placed for most family outings. Children can eat from the breakfast buffet at no charge, two under-16s can stay for free in family rooms, and there are cots on demand.

Rooms with a view

London Marriott Hotel County Hall
▨ Southbank

Westminster Bridge Road; tel: 020 798 5200; www.marriottcountyhall.com; map p.122 A3; £££

Next to the London Eye and opposite the Houses of Parliament, this has to be one of the best-located hotels in London. County Hall, formerly the seat of local government, has been beautifully restored and this hotel has all mod cons including a 25-yard pool.

The Trafalgar
▨ St James's

2 Spring Gardens; tel: 020 7870 2900; www1.hilton.com; map p.67 F5; ££

Not all the rooms in this chic boutique hotel have a view across Trafalgar Square. But all the rooms are spacious and have cosy armchairs, and if you go up to the roof terrace you will be eye to eye with Nelson on his column.

Swissôtel The Howard
▨ Covent Garden

Temple Place; tel: 020 7836 3555; www.swissotel.com; map p.85 F1; ££££

If you get a room at the front of this hotel you get amazing sweeping views of the river from the Houses of Parliament to St Paul's Cathedral. This efficient, friendly hotel is also well placed for theatres and the West End.

Essentials

A

Airports and arrival
(see also Public transport)

London has two major international airports: Heathrow, 15 miles (24km) to the west, and Gatwick, 25 miles (40km) to the south, plus three smaller airports, Stansted and Luton to the north and London City to the east.

Heathrow: The fastest connection to central London is the Heathrow Express (tel: 0845 600 1515; www.heathrowexpress.com) to Paddington station, which runs every 15 minutes between around 5am and 11.45pm, taking 15 minutes. Paddington then connects with several tube lines (see map p.192) . A cheaper option is the 25-minute Heathrow Connect service (tel: 08457 484 950; www.heathrowconnect.com). There is a direct tube route on the Piccadilly line, which reaches central London in 50 minutes, via Kensington and Piccadilly to King's Cross, and operates daily from 5am (6am on Sun) until 11.40pm.

National Express (tel: 08717 818 181; www.nationalexpress.com) runs coaches from Heathrow's central bus station to Victoria Coach Station; journey time 45–80 minutes.

Gatwick: The Gatwick Express (tel: 0845 850 1530; www.gatwickexpress.com) leaves Gatwick for Victoria Station every 15 minutes, 4.35am–1.35am. It takes 30 minutes. You can also take non-express services to Victoria and King's Cross, which are a bit cheaper and take 35–45 minutes.

National Express runs coaches from Gatwick's bus station to Victoria Coach Station; journey time around 90 minutes. Information, as above.

Stansted: The Stansted Express (tel: 0800 028 2878; www.stanstedexpress.com) direct rail link goes to Liverpool Street Station every 15 minutes; average journey time 45 minutes.

National Express runs coaches from Stansted to Oxford Street and Victoria Coach Station; journey time around 90 minutes. Information, as above.

London City: The DLR stop for London City Airport is six minutes from Canning Town tube (Jubilee line), running every 10 minutes from 5.30am–1.15am.

Luton: Luton Airport Parkway rail is linked by Thameslink services to King's Cross and Blackfriars, taking 40 minutes and running around every 15 minutes on weekdays only.

National Express runs coaches from Luton to Oxford Street and Victoria Coach Station; journey time around 90 minutes. Information, as above.

Airport numbers

Heathrow, tel: 0844 335 1801
Gatwick, tel: 0844 335 1802
Luton, tel: 01582 405 100
Stansted, tel: 0870 000 0303
London City, tel: 020 7646 0088

Arrival by train

Eurostar services from Paris Gare du Nord take around 2¼ hours (Paris, tel:

0033 8 92 35 35 39), and from Brussels 2 hours (Brussels, tel: 0032 25 28 28 28) to the terminal at London St Pancras. For UK bookings, tel: 08432 186 186; for bookings from abroad 01233 617 575. Also visit www.eurostar.com.

Vehicles are also carried by **Le Shuttle** trains through the tunnel between Folkestone in Kent and Sangatte in France. There are two to five departures each hour, and the trip takes 35 minutes. Bookings are not essential, but advisable at peak times. Fares vary according to the time of travel and how far in advance you book: late at night or early morning are usually cheaper. For information and reservations tel: 08443 353 535 (UK), 0810 63 03 04 (France) or from any other country 00 33 (0)3 2100 2061, or visit www.eurotunnel.com.

C
Climate
London's climate is generally mild all year round. Snow is unusual, and January temperatures average 6°C (43°F). Temperatures in the summer months average 18°C (64°F), but they can soar, causing the city to become very stuffy. It often rains, so keep an umbrella handy at all times.

D
Disabled access
An excellent guidebook is *Access in London* (Quiller Press). The London Tourist Board also provides a free leaflet, *London For All*, available from Information Centres. For details on public transport pick up *Access to the Underground* (free from ticket offices) and Transport for London's *Access to Mobility* (www.tfl.gov.uk). Artsline is a free telephone and online information service for disabled people in London, covering the arts and entertainment (tel: 020 7388 2227; www.artsline.org.uk), Mon–Fri 9.30am–5.30pm.

Driving
Unless you are planning on making several trips outside the capital, a car is most likely to be more of a hindrance than a help, and certainly a considerable expense, owing to the congestion charge (*see below*) and the high cost of parking. If you are driving, be sure to observe the speed limits (police detection cameras are increasingly common).

Congestion charge: Cars driving into a clearly marked Congestion Zone, extending between Kensington and the City, between 7am and 6.30pm Mon–Fri are filmed, and their drivers are fined if a payment of £8 has not been made by midnight the same day (or £10 the following day). You can pay at many small shops, including newsagents, by phone (tel: 0845 900 1234) or at www.cclondon.com.

Parking: This is a big problem in congested central London. Meters are slightly less expensive than NCP (multistorey) car parks, but some only allow parking for a maximum of two hours; it can also be hard to find a free one. Most meter parking is free after 6.30pm daily, after 1.30pm in most areas on Saturday, and all day Sunday, but always check this on the meter.

E
Embassies
Australia: Australia House, Strand, WC2B 4LA; tel: 020 7379 4334
Canada: Macdonald House, 1 Grosvenor Square, W1X 4AB; tel: 020 7258 6600
Ireland: 17 Grosvenor Place, SW1X 7HR; tel: 020 7235 2171
New Zealand: 80 Haymarket, SW1Y 4TQ; tel: 020 7930 8422
US: 24 Grosvenor Square, W1A 1AE; tel: 020 7499 9000

Emergencies
For police, fire brigade or ambulance dial 999 from any telephone (no money or card required) and tell the operator which service you require.

G
Gay and lesbian
With Europe's largest gay and lesbian population, London has an abundance of bars, restaurants and clubs to cater for most tastes, with the scene focusing around Soho, Earl's Court and Vauxhall. For listings, consult the free gay weekly magazines, *Boyz*, the *Pink Paper* and *QX*. Monthly magazines for sale include *Gay Times*,

Diva and *Attitude*.

Useful telephone contacts for advice and counselling include London Lesbian and Gay Switchboard (tel: 020 7837 7324) and London Friend (7.30–10pm; tel: 020 7837 3337).

H
Health and medical care
EU citizens can receive free treatment on producing a European Health Insurance Card; citizens of other countries must pay, except for emergency treatment (always free). Major hospitals include :
Charing Cross Hospital (Fulham Palace Road, W6; tel: 020 8846 1234), University College London Hospitals (Huntley Street, W1; tel 020 7387 9300) and St Thomas's (Lambeth Palace Road, SE1; tel: 020 7188 7188). Guy's Hospital Dental Department is at St Thomas Street, SE1; tel: as before 020 7188 7188. For the nearest hospital or doctor's, ring NHS Direct, tel: 0845 46 47. Late pharmacy: Bliss Chemist, 5 Marble Arch, W1, opens till midnight.

I
Internet
Free Wi-fi internet access is increasingly common in London, in coffee shops, hotels, pubs and bookstores. Pay-as-you-go internet access is available at many venues including the easy chain, www.easyinternetcafe.com.

L

Left luggage

Most of the capital's main railway stations have left-luggage departments where you can leave your suitcases on a short-term basis, although all are extremely sensitive to potential terrorist bombs. Left-luggage offices close at around 10pm (including St Pancras) or 11pm, with the exception of Victoria, which remains open until midnight.

Lost property

For possessions lost on public transport or in taxis, contact Transport for London's central Lost Property, 200 Baker Street, NW1 5RZ (tel: 0845 330 9882), Mon–Fri 8.30am–4pm, or fill in an enquiry form, available from any London Underground station or bus garage. If you lose your passport, let your embassy know as well as the nearest police station (for numbers of these, call directory enquiries on 118 500, 118 888 or 118 811).

M

Maps

For detailed exploration of the city centre and suburbs, the London A–Z books, with all roads indexed, come in various formats. Free tube maps are available at Underground stations.

Money

Banks: These usually open 9.30am–4.30/5pm Monday to Friday, with Saturday-morning banking common in shopping areas. Major English banks tend to offer similar exchange rates, so it is only worth looking around if you have large amounts of money to change. Currency exchange is offered at main post office branches and is commission free.

ATMs: The easiest way to take out currency is using an ATM. There are myriad cash machines across London, inside and outside banks, in supermarkets and at rail and tube stations. They operate on global credit and debit systems including Maestro/Cirrus, Switch, Visa and others.

Credit cards: International credit cards are almost universally accepted in shops, restaurants, hotels etc.

Museums and galleries

Although national museums and galleries are free, most others have entrance charges. Energetic visitors will benefit from the **London Pass**, which allows free entry to several dozen attractions. Free travel on the tube and buses is also included. For details tel: 01664 485 020 or check www.londonpass.com.

Joining the Art Fund costs around £40 a year and provides free admission to more than 200 museums, galleries and historic houses around the country, plus discounts on some exhibitions. Details on 0870 848 2003 or from www.artfund.org.

N

Newspapers and listings

Daily national papers include the *Daily Telegraph* and *The Times* (both on the right politically), *The Independent* (in the middle) and *The Guardian* (left of centre). Most have Sunday equivalents. The *Financial Times* is more business and finance orientated. Except for the *Daily Mirror*, the tabloids (*The Sun, Star, Daily Mail, Daily Express* and *Metro*) are right-wing.

The free *Evening Standard* and *Metro* (Mon–Fri), given away at stations, are good for cinema and theatre listings. For the most comprehensive, up-to-the-minute listings go to www.timeout.com/london.

P

Postal services

Most post offices open Mon–Fri 9am–5pm, Sat 9am–noon. London's main post office (24-8 William IV Street; Mon, Wed–Fri 8.30am–6.30pm, Tue open from 9.15am, Sat 9am–5.30pm) is by Trafalgar Square, behind the church of St Martin-in-the-Fields.

Postcodes

The first half of London postcodes indicates the general area (WC = West Central, SE = South East) and the second half, used only for mail, identifies the exact block. Here is a key to some of the commoner codes:

W1 Mayfair, Marylebone, Soho; W2 Bayswater; W4 Chiswick; W8 Kensington; W11 Notting Hill; WC1 Bloomsbury; WC2 Covent Garden, Strand; E1 Whitechapel; EC1 Clerkenwell; EC2 Bank, Barbican; EC4 St Paul's, Blackfriars; SW1 St James's, Belgravia; SW3 Chelsea; SW7 Knightsbridge, South Kensington; SW19 Wimbledon; SE1 Lambeth, Southwark; SE10 Greenwich; SE21 Dulwich; N1 Hoxton, Islington; N6 Highgate; NW3 Hampstead.

Public holidays

1 Jan: New Year's Day
Mar/Apr: Good Fri; Easter Mon
May: May Day (first Mon of month); Spring Bank Holiday (last Mon)
Aug: Summer Bank Holiday (last Mon of month)
25 Dec: Christmas Day
26 Dec: Boxing Day

Public transport

Tickets and fares

London's transport map is divided into six zones, spreading outwards from central London (zones 1–2) to cover all of Greater London. Tube and rail fares are priced according to which zones you travel in. Single tickets on London's transport networks are very expensive, so it's best to buy one of several multi-journey passes. **Travel cards** give unlimited travel on the tube, buses and DLR. Off-peak travel cards (valid after 9.30am) are considerably cheaper. You can also buy three-day or seven-day cards.

Oyster cards are smart cards that you charge up with credit (using cash or a credit card), then touch in on card readers at tube stations, buses and some railway stations (see *Rail*), so that an amount is deducted each time you use it. They are cheaper than travel cards if you only expect to travel a few times each day. Cards and Oysters can be bought from tube and DLR stations and newsagents. Visitors can order them ahead from www.visitbritaindirect.com.

Under-11s travel free on the tube and DLR at off-peak times provided they are with an adult. Otherwise, Travelcards for children aged 5–15 are available at a special reduced rate. Children under 16 travel for free at all times on buses, but 14- to 15-year-olds need a 14–15 Oyster photocard.

For full details of all fares, see www.tfl.gov.uk.

Underground (tube)

The fastest and easiest way to get around London is by tube. Try to avoid the rush hours (8am–9.30am and 5–6.30pm), when trains are packed with commuters. Services run from 5.30am to just after midnight. Make sure you have a ticket and keep hold of it after you have passed through the barrier; you will need it to exit. Oyster cards (*see above*) are a wise buy if you plan to travel a lot by tube. For enquiries, tel: 020 7222 1234; www.tfl.gov.uk.

Docklands Light Railway

The DLR runs from Bank and Tower Gateway to east and southeast London destinations. Tickets are the same type and cost as for the tube.

Rail

London's commuter rail network provides links to areas not on underground lines. Travelcards are still valid on rail services for journeys within the correct zones. Oyster cards can only be used on London Overground stations (*see below*). These are the principal mainline stations, with the areas of London and the rest of the country they serve:

Charing Cross Station. Services to south London and southeast England: Canterbury, Folkestone, Hastings, Dover Priory.

Euston Station. Services to northwest London and beyond to Birmingham and the northwest: Liverpool, Manchester, Glasgow.

King's Cross Station. Services to north London and beyond to the northeast: Leeds, York, Newcastle, Edinburgh and Aberdeen.

St Pancras Station. Points not quite so far north, such as Nottingham, Derby and Sheffield, and the new Eurostar terminal for trains from Paris and Brussels.

Liverpool Street Station and **Fenchurch Street**. To east and northeast London, Cambridge and East Anglia.

Paddington Station. Services to west London and to Oxford, Bath, Bristol, the west, and South Wales.

Victoria Station. Services to south

London and southeast England, including Gatwick Airport, Brighton, Newhaven and Dover.

Waterloo Station. To southwest London, Southampton, and southern England as far as Exeter, including Richmond, Windsor and Ascot. Other terminals, such as **Marylebone**, **London Bridge**, **Cannon Street** and **Blackfriars**, are mainly commuter stations, used for destinations around London.

Thameslink services run through the city centre, while the **London Overground** connects Richmond to Stratford, via the north of the capital, and Dalston Junction to West Croydon – connecting southeast to northeast London on the newly extended East London line.

For times and enquiries; tel: 0845 748 4950; www.nationalrail.co.uk.

Bus

If you are not in a hurry, travel by bus provides a good way of seeing London; the bus network is very comprehensive. The flat fare is £2. Again, an Oyster card is the best bet, as each journey then costs £1.20, and the total is price-capped at £3.90 per day. Night buses run all night on the most popular routes. Full bus route maps are available at Travel Information Centres.

Boat

River cruises are a great way to see London's sights, and various routes run on the Thames between Hampton Court and Barrier Gardens. There is a hop-on-hop-off River Rover pass; see www.citycruises.com.

T

Taxis

Black cabs are licensed and display the charges on the meter. They can be hailed in the street if their 'for hire' sign is lit. There are also ranks at major train stations and at various points across the city, or you can order a cab on 0871 871 8710. Black cabs are licensed to carry up to five people (six in the special Metrocabs and Mercedes Vitos) plus luggage. There are no additional charges for extra passengers or items of luggage within these limits. All black cabs are wheelchair accessible.

There is an additional charge when you take a black cab from Heathrow Airport and when you book a black cab by telephone. Many black cabs accept payment by credit or debit card (for an additional charge), but check with the driver before the trip starts.

You can tip taxi drivers as much as you like, but most people round up to the nearest pound.

Minicabs should only be hired by phone; they are not allowed to pick up passengers on the street. Reputable firms include: Addison Lee, tel: 020 7387 8888; www.addisonlee.com.

Telephones

London's UK dialling code is 020. To call from abroad, dial '44', the international access code for Britain, then 20 (the London code, with the initial '0' dropped), then the individual number.

Useful numbers

Emergency – police, fire, ambulance: tel: 999
Operator (for difficulties in getting through): tel: 100
International Operator: tel: 155
Directory Enquiries (UK): tel: 118 500 or 118 888 or 118 811
International Directory Enquiries: tel: 118 505 or 118 866 or 118 899

Theatre tickets

The only way to get a ticket at face value is to buy it from the theatre box office. Most open 10am–mid-evening. You can pay by credit card over the phone for most theatres, or reserve seats three days in advance before paying. A ticket booth (TKTS) on the south side of Leicester Square offers unsold seats at half price or three-quarter price (plus booking fee) on the day of performance (Mon–Sat 10am–7pm, Sun noon–3pm). Two reputable 24-hour agents are Keith Prowse at 0844 209 0382 and Ticket-master at www.ticketmaster.co.uk.

Time

In winter, Great Britain is on Greenwich Mean Time, which is 8 hours ahead of Los Angeles, 5 hours ahead of New York and Montreal, and 10 hours behind Sydney. During the summer, from the last Sunday in March to the last Sunday in October, clocks are put forward one hour.

Tourist offices

The official tourist board (www.visit london.com) offers information on sights, events and practical points, plus a commercial hotel booking service. Personal enquiries can be made at Britain and London Visitor Centre, 1 Regent Street, Piccadilly Circus, SW1Y 4XT (Mon 9.30am–6.30pm, Tue–Fri 9am–6.30pm, Sat–Sun 10am–4pm, except June–Sept Sat 9am–5pm).

There are other tourist information centres in the City (St Paul's Churchyard; tel: 020 7332 1456); Greenwich (Pepys House, 2 Cutty Sark Gardens; tel: 0870 608 2000) and on the South Bank (Vinopolis, 1 Bank End; tel: 020 7357 9168).

W

Websites

In addition to the many websites listed in this guidebook, the following are useful for information on London: www.bbc.co.uk/london (BBC London) www.thisislondon.co.uk (*Evening Standard* site; useful listings) www.metro.co.uk (*Metro* newspaper) www.london-se1.co.uk (information on the South Bank and Bankside) www.streetmap.co.uk (address locator) www.24hourmuseum.co.uk (up-to-date information on museum shows) www.timeout.com/london (for up-to-the-minute news and listings on cultural events across the capital).

Index

index

190

Insight Select Guide: London
Written by: Bridget Freer
Edited by: Cathy Muscat
Layout by: Ian Spick
Maps: James Macdonald
Picture Manager: Steven Lawrence
Series Editor: Cathy Muscat

Photography: All pictures by APA Ming Tang
Evans except: Phil Ashley/St Martin-in-the-Fields
71; AWL Images 151; Axiom 33; The Berkeley 153;
Mathew Booth 152; Britain on View 129; Natae
Carioni 43; Charlotte Street Hotel 41; Courtesy of
the Connaught 42; Samuel Courtauld Trust, The
Courtauld Gallery, London 58; Dean and Chapter
of Westminster 81; Design Centre Chelsea Harbour
148; Courtesy the Chelsea Physic Garden 155;
Design Museum 122; Courtesy Donmar Warehouse
56; Paul Downey 57; Food52 105; Fotolia 98; Fotolibra
60; Getty Images 35, 59, 75, 121; Marcus Ginns 149;
Hakkasan 7B; Hemis/Photolibrary 133, 164–165;
Historic Royal Palaces 76; Mandarin Oriental 154;
Mathew Hollow 30; Courtesy of the Howard 38–39;
Imperial War Museum 77; Istockphoto 3B, 31, 52,
136; Lesley Craze Gallery 99; South Molton Street
Association 29; Ewan Munro 95; Courtesy the
Newman Arms 88; John Offenbach 150; The Old
Operating Theatre 132; PA Photos 15; Photolibrary
64; Courtesy the Photographers Gallery 63; Pictures
Colour Library 50; Courtesy Pollocks Toy Museum
99; The Royal Exchange 119; Sevendials.co.uk 62;
Courtesy of Sketch 34; Peter Smith 110; Sir John
Soans Museum 91; Andy Spain 112; Superstock 87,
106–107, 114; The Tate 72; Angus Taylor 55; John
Tramper 131; Courtesy of Geo. F. Trumper 36; United
Grand Lodge of England 61; Visit London 10, 13B,
82, 115, 161; Michael Walter 90; Courtesy Whitechapel Art Gallery 109; Wigmore Hall 27; The Wolseley
26; V&A Images 146; Vertigo 42, 111

Cartography: Maps reproduced by permission of
Geographers' A–Z Map Co. Ltd. Licence No. B4867.
© Crown Copyright 2010. All Rights Reserved.
Licence number 100017302. Pages 20-21 Derived
from Meridian2 data © Crown copyright

First Edition 2010
Reprinted 2011
© 2010 Apa Publications GmbH & Co.
Verlag KG Singapore Branch, Singapore.
Printed in Germany
Distribution:
Distributed in the UK and Ireland by:
GeoCenter International Ltd
Meridian House, Churchill Way West, Basingstoke,
Hampshire RG21 6YR; tel: (44 1256) 817 987; email:
sales@geocenter.co.uk
Distributed in the United States by:
Ingram Publisher Services
One Ingram Blvd, PO Box 3006
La Vergne, TN 37086-1986; email: customer.
service@ingrampublisherservices.com
Distributed in Australia by:
Universal Publishers
PO Box 307, St. Leonards, NSW 1590;
email: sales@universalpublishers.com.au
Distributed in New Zealand by:
Hema Maps New Zealand Ltd (HNZ)
Unit 2, 10 Cryers Road, East Tamaki, Auckland
2013; email: sales.hema@clear.net.nz
Worldwide distribution by:
APA Publications GmbH & Co Verlag KG (Sin-
gapore branch); 7030 Ang Mo Kio Ave 5; 08-65
Northstar @ AMK; Singapore 569880; apasin@
signet.com.sg

Contacting the Editors
We would appreciate it if readers would alert us to
outdated information by writing to:
Apa Publications, PO Box 7910, London SE1 1WE,
UK; email: insight@apaguide.co.uk
No part of this book may be reproduced, stored in
a retrieval system or transmitted in any form or by
any means (electronic, mechanical, photocopying,
recording or otherwise), without prior written
permission of Apa Publications. Brief text quota-
tions with use of photographs are exempted for
book review purposes only. Information has been
obtained from sources believed to be reliable, but its
accuracy and completeness, and the opinions based
thereon, are not guaranteed.

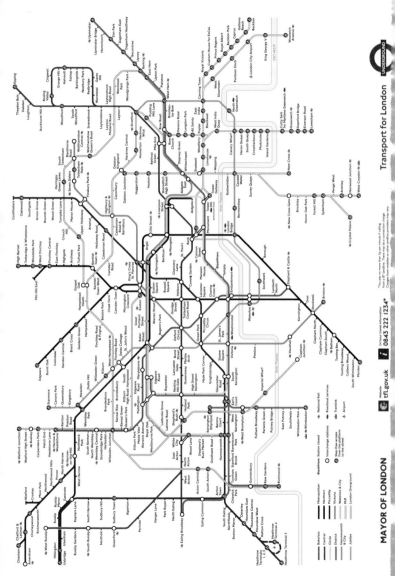

MAYOR OF LONDON

Transport for London

UNDERGROUND

192